The
Babyproofing Bible

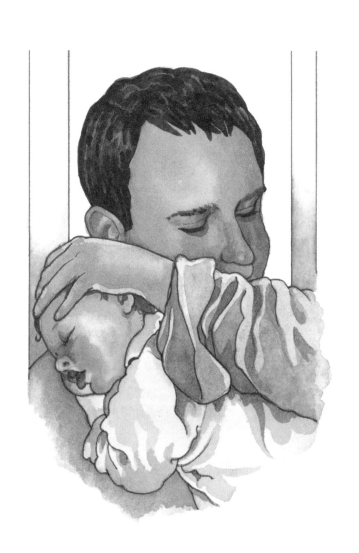

The
Babyproofing Bible

THE EXCEEDINGLY THOROUGH GUIDE
TO KEEPING YOUR CHILD SAFE

From Crib to Kitchen to Car to Yard

Jennifer Bright Reich

FAIR WINDS
PRESS
BEVERLY, MASSACHUSETTS

First published in the USA in 2007 by
Fair Winds Press, a member of
Quayside Publishing Group
100 Cummings Center
Suite 406-L
Beverly, MA 01915-6101

11 10 09 08 07   1 2 3 4 5

ISBN-13: 978-1-59233-248-9
ISBN-10: 1-59233-248-X

Library of Congress Cataloging-in-Publication Data

Reich, Jennifer Bright.
    The babyproofing bible: the exceedingly thorough guide to keeping your child safe from crib to kitchen to car to yard / Jennifer Bright Reich.

        p. cm.

    Includes index.

ISBN 1-59233-248-X

1. Children's accidents--Prevention. 2. Home accidents --Prevention.
3. Infants--Care. 4. Child-rearing--Safety measures. I. Title.

HV675R45 2007

613.6--dc22

                2007016361

Cover and book design by Rachel Fitzgibbon
Illustrations by Wendy Edelson

Printed and bound in China

To Mike, Tyler, and Austin

Contents

INTRODUCTION

Your baby is counting on you—for love, laughter, learning, and also for safety. I'll bet you've got the three Ls covered, and this book is going to get you up to speed on the safety part.

In a bit of serendipity, I wrote this book as I was actually babyproofing my own home. My older son had just turned six months old and was trying to crawl and stand up. All of a sudden the dishwashing detergent under the sink, the miniblind cords dangling from the windows, and the picture frames on the bottom shelf of the bookcase no longer seemed like good ideas, and my husband and I started babyproofing in earnest.

But although this process has given me real-life experience, I'm not an expert on every aspect of babyproofing, so I consulted real experts as well. I talked with government safety experts, nonprofit safety organization founders, pediatricians, teachers, and dozens of parents to glean their proven, time-tested tips.

As I gathered the tips for this book, I focused on ideas that you can implement quickly. This book shows you how to make the huge task of babyproofing your home manageable by breaking it up into smaller chunks.

But safety is a serious subject, and in no way does the quick-tip aspect of this book intend to trivialize it. Accidents are the leading cause of death for children. According to the U.S. Consumer Product Safety Commission, about two and one-half million children are injured or killed each year by dangers in their own homes. Babyproofing is a critical task, not to be taken lightly.

Because babies learn and grow so quickly, babyproofing is a constantly evolving process, not a once-and-done project. As your baby grows, you need to continue to make changes to your home. That's why this book is designed to anticipate your baby's growing needs. For example, the gate you install to keep your one-year-old from venturing up the stairs might become an invitation to climb when he's two. So this book is broken up into several parts, based on your baby's age.

Part I offers advice on preparing your home for your new baby. It includes tips on getting the nursery ready, for buying baby gear, and for making changes throughout the house.

Part II talks about safety for your baby from birth to six months, before he starts crawling. It includes advice for every room in the house, including the nursery, kitchen, bathroom, living room, and even outside.

Part III takes you from six months to one year, when your baby is crawling and later standing, but not yet walking. Part IV picks up at the toddler years, when your baby is walking. These two parts also go room by room though your home: the nursery, kitchen, bathroom, living room, and outside. And finally, part V talks about taking your baby out in cars, to other people's homes, and to other places you might explore.

As you read this book and babyproof your home, please keep in mind that all of the babyproofing in the world is no substitute for watchful parenting. If you sense that something is not right with your baby, *check him right away.* The most powerful piece of safety equipment you possess is your instinct.

Best wishes to you and your baby for a lifetime of happiness, health, and safety.

PART I

Preparing
for Your
BABY

WHEN YOU FIRST SEE THE TWO LINES APPEAR LIKE MAGIC ON THE PREGNANCY TEST OR HEAR THE DOCTOR ANNOUNCE, "YOU'RE PREGNANT!" YOUR LIFE CHANGES. IT'S LIKE WHEN THEY FLIP THE SWITCH ON A TRAIN TRACK, CHANGING THE TRAIN'S DIRECTION FROM ONE PATH TO ANOTHER. SUDDENLY THE WORLD IS A DIFFERENT PLACE; YOU NOTICE OTHER PREGNANT WOMEN EVERYWHERE, CHILDREN SEEM MUCH MORE INTERESTING, AND EVERYTHING LOOKS A LITTLE BRIGHTER.

THEN PANIC SETS IN. YOU HAVE ABOUT A MILLION THINGS TO DO, AND LESS THAN NINE MONTHS TO DO THEM. IT'S LIKE THE BEGINNING OF A RACE. CERTAINLY RIGHT UP THERE AT THE TOP OF YOUR TO-DO LIST IS MAKING YOUR HOME SAFE FOR YOUR BABY. "SAFE"—SUCH A SMALL WORD FOR SUCH A HUGE RESPONSIBILITY. BUT LIKE ANY IMPORTANT UNDERTAKING, BABYPROOFING CAN BE BROKEN DOWN INTO SMALL STEPS. AND BECAUSE YOUR BABY WON'T BE MOBILE FOR AWHILE, YOU'RE AT LEAST A FEW STEPS AHEAD OF HER!

IN THIS PART, WE'LL TALK ABOUT SETTING UP YOUR BABY'S NURSERY, BUYING HER BABY GEAR, AND BABYPROOFING THE REST OF THE HOUSE. THE RACE HAS BEGUN—READY, SET, GO!

The Nursery

Even just thinking about your baby's nursery probably makes you smile. Tiny onesies, booties, and hats; stacks of diapers, towels, and cloths; and baskets of toys, stuffed animals, and rattles all await your little one. You're taking great care to make your baby's nursery special. Now here's how to make your baby's nursery safe.

Choosing the Safest Crib

Your baby's crib is a very important purchase. Choose wisely for his sweet dreams.

- Be wary of used cribs. Older cribs may be weak with age, covered with lead-based paint, or fail to meet today's safety standards. According to Kids in Danger, an organization dedicated to improving children's product safety, cribs more than five years old are too old to reuse.
- Make sure the crib has a label stating it meets the U.S. Consumer Product Safety Commission's standards.
- Look for a crib with Juvenile Product Manufacturers Association (JPMA) certification as well.
- Stay away from crib models with attached dressers. Later on, your baby could use the dresser to scale out of the crib and fall.
- Be sure the space between crib slats in less than 2 $^3/_8$ inches (6 cm). The slats should be close enough together that a soda can won't fit between them.
- Never use a crib that has loose or missing slats.
- Make sure the wood has no splinters or cracks.
- Because a baby's clothing can become snagged on high corner posts, the posts should not be higher than $^1/_{16}$ inch (1 mm) above the top of the top rail. Or they should be very tall, such as posts on a canopy bed. Remove any decorative knobs on corner posts.
- Avoid cribs with headboard and footboard cutout designs that could allow the baby to become trapped.
- Check that the mattress support hangers are secured by bolts or closed hooks.
- Make sure all crib hardware is tightened securely.
- The mattress should adjust up and down, and its highest setting should be no more than 26 inches (66 cm) from the top of the railing.
- Make sure that when the crib sides are lowered, they are at least 9 inches (22.5 cm) above the mattress support to keep your baby from falling out.
- Check that the crib's drop-side latches hold the sides up securely and can't be lowered by your baby or released by accident.

Assemble with care. Take your time to assemble the crib correctly. Make sure that all hardware is properly in place. If you're not comfortable putting the crib together yourself, ask someone who is to do it for you.

Consider location. Place your baby's crib away from windows and radiators.

Be firm. Choose a firm mattress. Your baby shouldn't sink into it. Of the two types of crib mattresses—foam and innerspring—higher-priced models tend to be firmer, and therefore safer. Give the mattress a squeeze test.

Check the fit. It you can fit more than two fingers between the mattress and crib, the mattress is too small. Your baby could get stuck between the mattress and crib sides and suffocate.

Find another use for that comforter. Many baby bedding sets come with comforters, but they pose a suffocation risk. Keep yours out of the crib and don't drape it over the side rails or hang it on the wall above the crib where your baby could reach it.

Think twice about bumper pads. Sure, they look adorable, and our image of the perfect crib is encircled by soft, fluffy bumper pads, but safety experts warn that a baby's face can press up against them, limiting his breathing. Also, they obstruct your view of your baby inside the crib.

Fasten bumper pads securely. If you use bumper pads, make sure that they fit around the entire crib without gaps and that they tie or snap at least in each corner, in the middle of each long side, and on both the top and bottom edges. Trim off any excess fabric ties to keep your baby from getting tangled in them.

Check the sheets. Crib sheets must fit the mattress snugly so there's no loose material and the sheets can't slip off. The sheet must overlap the mattress so that when you pull on a corner of the sheet, it doesn't come off the mattress. Choose crib sheets that are fitted with elastic all the way around. Each time you wash the sheets, make sure they still fit well, as sheets can shrink in the dryer.

Accept no substitutes. Never use an adult sheet on a crib mattress. It can come loose, and your baby can become entangled in it.

THE CRIB

Ensure that all parts of the crib are very firmly secured, including extra add-ons such as a mobile.

Empty is best: Quilts, pillows, toys, and even bumpers can put your baby at risk for suffocation.

Even in its raised position, the mattress should never be closer than 26 inches to the top of the crib.

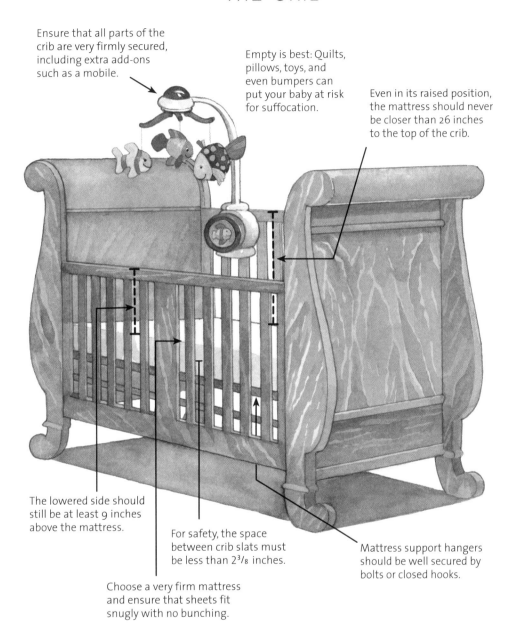

The lowered side should still be at least 9 inches above the mattress.

For safety, the space between crib slats must be less than $2^3/_8$ inches.

Choose a very firm mattress and ensure that sheets fit snugly with no bunching.

Mattress support hangers should be well secured by bolts or closed hooks.

Your baby's crib is the first and most important piece of furniture that you will need to evaluate for safety. Avoid hand-me-down cribs that may be worn out or could have been made according to outdated manufacturing safety standards.

Shelve the menagerie. Keep stuffed animals and toys out of your baby's crib. Store them on a high shelf away from the crib and out of your baby's reach.

Place nightlights right. Plug nightlights into outlets that are at least 3 feet (1 m) from the crib, bedding, and draperies to prevent a fire.

Arrange it right. "Arrange the furniture in your baby's nursery so there's a straight shot from his crib to his changing table," said Shalena Smith, owner of Ga Ga Designs, a Los Angeles–based interior design company that specializes in nurseries and kids' rooms. "In the middle of the night, you'll often need to pick up a crying, wet baby from his crib and carry him to his changing table. You don't want to trip over the rocking chair or anything else along the way."

Think small. "If possible, avoid tall bookcases and armoires in your nursery," said Smith. "Design the room not just for the newborn, but with the feisty toddler in mind, who might try to climb the bookcase to get to things on high shelves. If you must have a high bookcase, be sure to bolt it to the walls." (Thirty-three inches [84 cm] or lower in height is optimal bookshelf height.)

Check toys carefully. As you receive toys for your baby, look them over carefully to make sure they're in good condition. Check that they have no buttons, eyes, beads, ribbons, or other pieces that your baby could pull off and choke on. And don't underestimate a baby's strength. Even a newborn's grip is strong enough that he can briefly support his own weight. (Babies are born with a grasp reflex. Scientists hypothesize that human babies inherited this reflex from primates; the instinct to cling has survival benefits.)

Don't give your baby toys with strings that are more than 12 inches (30 cm) long. They could be a strangulation hazard. And always check the age recommendations on toys. Toys too advanced can pose safety hazards.

Don't use a toy without checking the instructions. Used toys, for example, likely came without the packaging that would give you age recommendations and instructions for safe use. Contact the manufacturer for a copy of the instructions.

CHOOSING THE SAFEST BASSINET

Perhaps you're getting a bassinet to use in your baby's nursery instead of a crib for his first few months, or perhaps it's for another room in the house. Here's how to buy with safety in mind:

- Look for a bassinet with a stable base. If it folds up, make sure the legs lock securely into place.
- Avoid rough or sharp edges.
- Make sure the mattress pad is less than 1½ inches (3.75 cm) thick, fits snugly against the bassinet's sides, and is firm.

CHOOSING THE SAFEST CHANGING TABLE

You'll be changing upward of 2,600 diapers in your baby's first year alone. Here's how to choose the safest changing table to get the job done safely:

- Make sure the table has four side rails. Changing tables are associated with 2,000 to 3,000 injuries each year, and many of them involve changing tables with only three side rails. A new industry standard will require changing tables to have rails on all four sides.
- Purchase a changing table that has guardrails at least 2 inches (5 cm) high on all sides. Four inches (10 cm) is even better.
- Make sure that the table has a safety strap. Or purchase one separately and install it yourself.
- Make note of the changing table's weight limit. They range from 20 to 30 pounds. A higher weight limit is a good indicator of stability.
- Buy a table with drawers or shelves that you can access while keeping one hand on your baby.
- Choose a table with a changing pad secured to the changing table's surface.
- Choose a changing table pad with contoured sides and a nonslip surface.

Wash toys. Wash new plastic toys in the top rack of your dishwasher or with a special toy cleaner. Then wash the toys on a regular basis. Some stuffed toys can be washed in the washing machine, but others can only be surface cleaned with a mix of water and mild detergent. Air dry them in a sunny spot indoors.

Consider a baby monitor. A baby monitor helps you keep tabs on what your baby is doing, which is especially important at night if your baby sleeps away from you. Consider an audio monitor that has blinking lights as well as relaying noises. That way you'll see the lights blink even if you can't hear the monitor, such as if you have to turn the volume down to take a phone call. Newer digital monitors have less static and don't pick up the neighbor's cell-phone chats, and they can alleviate your worries that neighbors will hear you singing lullabies to your baby. Choose a monitor that sounds if the batteries are low or if you're out of range.

Or get baby TV: A video monitor lets you also see how your baby is doing. A wall- or table-mounted camera transmits an image to a TV-set-like monitor.

A third option, movement sensors, are under-the-mattress pads that alert you when your baby's movement stops for more than 20 seconds. Bear in mind that none of these are medical devices.

THE CHANGING TABLE

Ideal guard rails are 4 inches high; however, they must be at least 2 inches high to meet minimum safety standards.

Four guard rails are a modern safety standard; do not use older models with only three sides.

4 inches

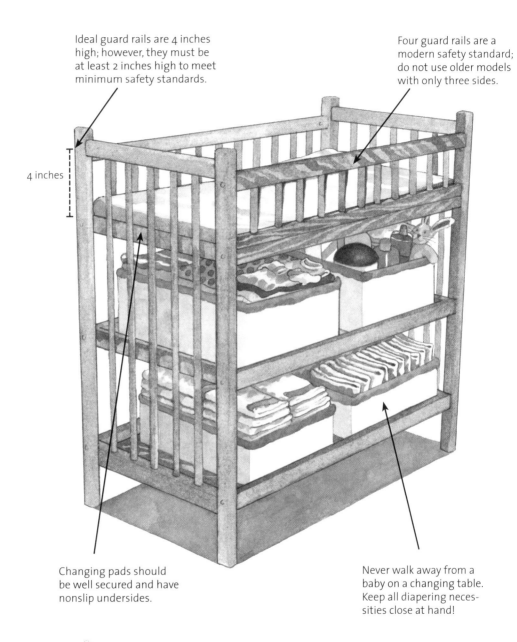

Changing pads should be well secured and have nonslip undersides.

Never walk away from a baby on a changing table. Keep all diapering necessities close at hand!

Thousands of infant injuries each year are connected to changing-table accidents. Make sure that your table is safely designed and that you use it with care.

Baby Gear

How can someone so small require so many things? Many parents-to-be buy baby gear before their babies are born—73 percent purchase every rattle, toy, and gizmo and 19 percent purchase only the essentials, according to a recent poll—so this section will discuss safety issues to consider when buying both essentials and extras. We'll talk about safe use in later sections, to correspond with when your baby begins using the items. We'll talk about one very important piece of baby gear—the car seat—in part V.

Check for recalls. "Most parents believe that when they buy a new product for their child, someone has made sure it is safe. This might not be true," says Nancy A. Cowles, director of Kids in Danger, a nonprofit organization dedicated to protecting children by improving children's product safety. "There is no requirement in the United States that children's products be tested for safety before they are sold. Because of that, an average of two children's products are recalled for safety issues each week. Even some *babyproofing products* have been recalled."

In 2006, 111 children's products—totaling almost nineteen million items—were recalled. But before they were recalled, they caused 177 injuries and six deaths.

Before using any new, and especially used, baby supplies, make sure the product hasn't been recalled by visiting the U.S. Consumer Product Safety Commission (CPSC) website www.cpsc.gov, calling them at 800-638-2772, or calling the manufacturer. Sign up on the CPSC website to receive e-mail alerts about product recalls.

Or check out www.recalls.gov, which was created by five federal regulatory agencies. It offers details about recalled products, safety information, follow-up instructions, and contact information.

Check for this seal. "Look for the Juvenile Products Manufacturers Association [JPMA] certification seal on baby products that you buy," says Amy Chezem, JPMA communications director. "The association works with organizations such as ASTM [American Society for Testing and Materials International] to conduct standards for seventeen categories of products, including strollers, changing tables, high chairs, infant carriers, and swings."

CHOOSING THE SAFEST SWING

Swings are popular with parents and babies alike because so many babies love them. Here's how to choose the safest one:

- Look for a sturdy swing with a wide base.
- Make sure it has safety straps.
- Check that the swing doesn't have any sharp edges.
- Check for small, removable parts that could be a choking hazard.

Do your homework. "Don't assume that something you buy is safe because someone is checking it," says Sue Chiang, the pollution prevention program director with the Center for Environmental Health (CEH). "For example, we have found lead in products such as soft vinyl lunchboxes and medicated baby powder. Think carefully about what kind of ingredients are in a product before you buy it." For more information about toxics found in consumer products, go to CEH's website, www.cehca.org.

Watch out for PVC. "Before buying plastic products for your baby, check for PVC, poly vinyl chloride, also referred to as 'vinyl,'" says Chiang. "These junk plastics contain heat stabilizers, which often are heavy metals such as lead." Sometimes these products state "PVC" on the label, and other times you might see the number 3 in the triangular recyclable symbol. More often though, it's not labeled at all.

Promptly send in warranty cards for products that you buy. If an item is recalled, the manufacturer needs your contact information to let you know.

Read the manual. And be sure to keep it in an accessible place.

Choosing the Safest Bouncer Seat

At first you'll want to hold your baby all of the time. But of course you do need to set her down sometimes so you can eat, shower, sleep, etc. A bouncer seat is the perfect tool for this job. Most babies love them.

- Look for a bouncer seat with anti-skid pads to keep it steady on the floor.
- Choose a seat with a base or rear support that's wider than the seat itself for steadiness.
- Test the seat's stability: Rock it front to back; it should stay in place. Press down on it from different positions; it shouldn't tip sideways.
- Test any interconnecting parts to make sure they won't accidentally loosen.
- If the bouncer has an attached toy bar, give the bar and toys a tug and a swat to make sure they don't pull off.

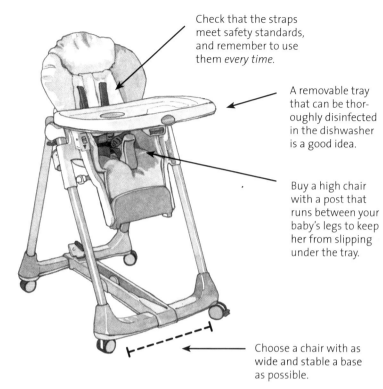

Check that the straps meet safety standards, and remember to use them *every time.*

A removable tray that can be thoroughly disinfected in the dishwasher is a good idea.

Buy a high chair with a post that runs between your baby's legs to keep her from slipping under the tray.

Choose a chair with as wide and stable a base as possible.

Choose a newer, safer high chair and use it with care.

CHOOSING THE SAFEST HIGH CHAIR

Each year four or five babies die from slipping under their high chair trays from not being properly strapped in. Here's how to choose a safe chair for your baby:

- Look for a high chair with a wide, stable base.
- Make sure the chair has both a safety strap that goes around your baby's waist and also between her legs. Ideally, you shouldn't be able to fasten one without the other.
- If possible, choose a high chair with a post to go between your baby's legs to keep her from slipping down under the tray.
- Check to be sure the caps or plugs on tubing are firmly attached.
- Consider a high chair with a tray and any teething toys that can go into the dishwasher for thorough cleanings.

Choosing the Safest Stroller

As far as indispensable baby gear goes, a stroller is pretty high on the list. Here are some safety things to keep in mind when buying yours:

- If the stroller has a basket for carrying packages, make sure the basket is low on the back of the stroller and directly over or in front of the rear wheels for proper balance.

- The stroller must have an adjustable five-point harness. Make sure the seat belt can be easily fastened.

- Check that the brake is easy to operate and securely locks the wheel. Better yet, choose a stroller with brakes on two wheels.

- For jogging strollers, choose one with a bicycle-style hand brake for slowing down and a foot-applied brake for parking.

- In the store, make sure you can safely open, close, and lift the stroller with one hand.

- Keep in mind that certain strollers are designed for specific ages. Carriage strollers fully recline, so they can be used for newborns on up. Strollers designed to work with infant car seats also can be used right away. Lightweight and all-terrain strollers usually can't be used until your baby is three months old. Some experts suggest waiting to use jogging strollers until babies are at least six months old, and even up to one year old, because the ride can be too bumpy for immature neck and spine muscles. And umbrella strollers, which don't have a lot of support, are for babies who can sit up on their own. This is usually six months at the earliest, when a baby has good trunk control.

- If you'll be off-roading it, choose a stroller with large wheels and a heavy-duty suspension.

CHOOSING THE SAFEST CARRIER

Carriers are wonderful alternatives to strollers, and babies love them because they get to be close to their parents. Carriers can be a lifesaver if you use public transportation a lot or in crowded stores where strollers are a nuisance.

There are several types of carriers, so when checking them out, make sure that the leg holes aren't too wide and that the interior isn't too rough. Test the straps to make sure they adjust easily and that they lock. Always follow the manufacturer's weight limits. If possible, test out the carrier before you buy it. Here are some specifics about the different types of carriers:

Baby slings are soft carriers for newborns on up. Some sling-type carriers for newborns convert into front carriers for older babies.

Front carriers are usually for babies at least 8 pounds (3.75 kg) and 21 inches (53.25 cm). Position your baby to ride facing you until her neck is strong enough to hold her head steady, which usually happens around three months.

Back carriers are for babies older than six months who are able to sit unassisted. Your baby needs to have adequate head and neck control to keep her head stable and unsupported. Framed carriers are terrific for walking or hiking. Look for the following:

- Make sure that it is deep enough to support your baby's back.
- Check that the leg openings are small enough to keep the baby from slipping out, but large enough that her legs won't become chafed.
- The pack should have a seat belt or safety harness.
- Ensure that there's padded covering over the metal frame to protect your baby from bumps.
- Look for a carrier with a sun shade.

Choosing the Safest Bathtub

You'll want to use a baby bathtub until your baby can sit up on her own, about the first six months.

- Look for a tub with supports that help keep your baby's head up.
- Consider a tub with a heat sensor that will warn you if the water is too hot. (If your tub doesn't have one, you can buy bath toys that change color in hot water.)
- Look for a tub with a comfortable cushion to keep your baby warm and secure.
- Check for a tub with a handy accessory tray for holding soap, shampoo, and a rinse pitcher. This is helpful to keep these things out of your baby's reach.

Choosing the Safest Play Yard

No longer called play pens, play yards are still very handy to keep babies contained—and safe.

- Choose a play yard with top rails that automatically lock when they are raised. (More than one million older models that had manually rotated top rail locks have been recalled.)
- Make sure the hardware doesn't protrude. (More than nine million older play pens with protruding hardware have been recalled.)
- Look for netting with a very small weave—less than 1/4 inch (5 mm). Also make sure the netting is free from tears or small holes, which could trap or injure an infant.
- Be sure the mesh is securely attached and that there are no missing or loose staples.

The raised mattress position cleverly allows the play yard to double as an infant bassinet.

Automatic locking rails are a must. Older models with rotating locks are *not* safe.

Netting should be secure all around and must have a very tight weave. Holes or tears in the netting could be dangerous.

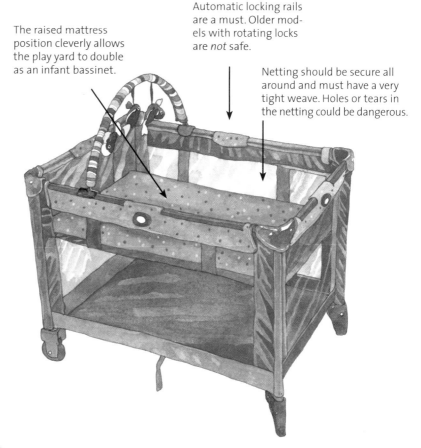

A play yard can be an important tool in keeping your baby safe as she gets older and more mobile. Be sure to select the right one with all the best safety features.

Report problems promptly. If you encounter any defect or problem, report it to the product manufacturer and the CPSC at www.cpsc.gov or 800-638-2772.

Beware of products made before 1970. Older items may have paints or finishes containing lead. Also keep in mind that federal safety standards didn't take effect until 1973.

Think twice about used gear. Old baby products may have broken or missing parts or not meet current safety guidelines. Plus it likely came without the packaging that would provide age recommendations and instructions for safe use. If you have thoroughly inspected an item and determined it is safe, call the manufacturer for a copy of the instructions or visit its website.

Throughout the House

It's true: Having a baby changes everything. Even before your baby comes home, your babyproofing needs to extend way beyond his nursery. Here's how to whip the rest of the house into baby-ready shape.

Post emergency numbers by each phone. Include the numbers for the fire department, police department, ambulance services (911 or the equivalent in your community), your baby's pediatrician's office and after-hours number, poison control (dialing 800-222-1222 will connect you to your local center), the closest hospital, and a neighbor.

Add your contact numbers, such as your work number and cell number and those of your partner, in case a babysitter needs to reach you. Also include your home address so that caregivers can easily tell emergency personnel where they are.

Make sure to let any babysitters know where the lists are. Tuck a copy of the numbers in your car, too.

Check into 911. In many U.S. communities, 911 is the number to call for the fire department, paramedics, and police, but not in all. Check your phone book to be sure.

Program emergency numbers into your cell phone. Include the numbers for the fire department, police department, ambulance services, your baby's pediatrician's office and after-hours number, poison control, and a neighbor.

Plan a route. Familiarize yourself with the route to the closest emergency room. You're likely doing this in anticipation of your baby's birth anyway, but once he's born, you'll be grateful that you know the quickest route if you ever need to get there fast.

Be prepared for emergencies. In case you need to rush your baby to the hospital, gather the following information together in an easy-to-grab emergency room file:

- Your family's health insurance identification numbers
- Phone numbers for your baby's pediatrician and pharmacist
- Directions to the nearest hospital emergency room

Be prepared. *The Babyproofing Bible* will help you to make your home safer and prevent accidents, but it's a good idea to also buy a first-aid/health book as a reference in case accidents occur.

Read medicine information each and every time. Get in the habit now of checking every medicine that you take—and later any you give to your baby—each and every time. Before you take a new medicine, read the information that accompanied it for side effects and drug interactions. Read the instructions carefully, especially the dosage and frequency information.

Infant CPR and First-Aid Classes

Taking a class on infant first aid and cardiopulmonary resuscitation (CPR) is extremely beneficial. Encourage your partner and anyone who might be baby-sitting your baby to do the same.

Don't want to leave the house? The Red Cross will send a certified instructor to your home to teach up to twelve adults. The cost is $25 to $40 per person, comparable to taking a regular class. To host a CPR party, go to www.redcross.org to find the number of your local Red Cross chapter.

ASSEMBLING A FIRST-AID KIT

Gather the following items into a plastic babyproof container:

- Acetaminophen
- Adhesive tape
- Antibiotic ointment
- Antiseptic cream such as bacitracin
- Antiseptic solution such as hydrogen peroxide
- Band-Aids
- Cotton
- Cotton swabs
- Disposable gloves
- Dosage spoon for medicine
- Flashlight with working batteries
- Hydrocortisone cream
- Scissors with blunt ends
- Sterile gauze
- Surgical tape
- Thermometer
- Tissues
- Tweezers

You can also purchase kits especially designed for new parents. Keep one kit in your home and a second in your car. Make it a habit to replace items right after you use them and check the expiration dates on products every so often. Tape a copy of your list of emergency numbers—fire, police, ambulance, poison control, pediatrician, and a neighbor—inside each kit.

Lower the water temperature in your home to 120°F (49°C). This will reduce the risk of being one of the approximately 3,800 injuries and thirty-four deaths that occur in homes each year because of scalding from excessively hot tap water. A child can get a third-degree burn from 140°F (60°C) water in just 3 seconds.

"Watch out for scalding, especially in the bathroom," says Garry Gardner, M.D., a pediatrician in private practice in Darien, Illinois, and former member of the American Academy of Pediatrics Committee on Injury, Violence, and Poison Prevention. "If you do the simple passive babyproofing of turning your hot water heater down to 120°F (49°C), it is almost impossible for a child to get third-degree burns from your hot water."

Test your water's temperature. Run your hot water until it's as hot as it gets. Fill a mug with hot water and check the temperature with a meat thermometer.

INSTALLING ANTI-SCALD DEVICES

Anti-scald devices, which cost around $90 not including installation, regulate your tap water temperature to prevent scald burns and cold-water shocks that can happen to someone running water when a toilet is flushed or another faucet is turned on. Anti-scald devices maintain water temperature at a safe level, despite fluctuations in water supply lines.

Unless you're a serious do-it-yourselfer, you might need to hire a plumber to install them. Put one on each faucet and showerhead.

Check smoke alarm placement. Each year more than 300 children ages five and younger die in fires. Smoke alarms cost as little as $10. You need one per floor, including the basement, and outside every sleeping area. If you sleep with the bedroom doors closed, install smoke alarms inside each bedroom as well.

Consider a vocal smoke alarm. Research has found that two out of three children sleep through a typical smoke alarm. But with a vocal smoke alarm, you record your own voice, which will wake your children more effectively if it goes off. You can even record a set of instructions.

Hush up. Consider installing a smoke alarm with a hush feature in places that often get false alarms, such as the kitchen. You can hit the hush button to silence a false alarm, which is far safer than taking out the batteries.

Test your alarms. Experts say that having a working smoke alarm can cut the chances of dying in a fire by half. Test your smoke alarms monthly. Follow the manufacturer's instructions. Usually you simply press the test button.

Get a second carrier. Consider getting a second, inexpensive baby carrier to keep in your baby's room. In case of a fire, put the baby into it to keep your hands free to exit and open doors.

Change the batteries. Replace the batteries in your smoke alarms at least once a year, such as when you change your clocks in October. And of course, change the batteries if they run low and the alarm starts to chirp.

Replace when needed. According to the National Fire Protection Association, fires kill more Americans each year than all natural disasters combined. Get new smoke alarms every ten years.

MAKING A FIRE ESCAPE PLAN

"A fire can spread through a home today in less than five minutes," says John Drengenberg, an electrical engineer and consumer affairs manager for Underwriters Laboratories (UL), a nonprofit product safety certification organization. "Have a fire evacuation plan and practice it. A few decades ago, home furnishings had more natural materials. Today, however, furnishings such as drapes, carpet, and furniture are largely made of synthetics, which burn much faster than natural materials. This causes fire to spread more quickly, plus these materials may release deadly fumes."

Gather everyone in your family and put together a fire escape plan. Talk about what you'll do in the event of a fire during daylight hours and at night. Teach your family that no matter how small the fire is, everyone must get out of the house and then you'll call the fire department. Remind your family to stay as close to the floor as possible as you escape. Walk through your home and note the most direct route out of the house from each room, and then identify at least two ways out of your home. Assign an adult to each child to help exit and consider how you will carry the child through a smoky room and practice it. Designate a safe, well-lit meeting place outside that's easy to remember, such as under a streetlight. Never go back inside a burning building.

Once you've put your plan together, test it with a family fire drill. Practice it at least twice a year.

Safety Supplies: Fire Escape Ladders

These collapsible ladders are a must if you live in a multi-story home. Keep one in each bedroom that's above the first floor. Store it under the bed, and then hook it onto the window you use to escape if smoke or flames block the door.

Make sure the ladder you buy fits your window ledges. Practice using it, preferably from a first floor window. Escape ladders cost around $40 at major retailers and through baby safety supplies catalogs.

Place fire extinguishers at key locations. A fire extinguisher can put out a small, contained fire before it can spread. Look for multipurpose extinguishers, which can put out all types of home fires. Have one on each floor; one in the kitchen, the garage, and the workshop; and one near fuel-burning appliances such as stoves, furnaces, and gas dryers.

Make sure that you know how and when to use the fire extinguisher. Your local fire department might offer training. Use a fire extinguisher only if someone else is able to get everyone out of the house safely and the fire is smaller than a small trash can. Keep your back to the exit in case you need to escape the fire's spread.

PASS. Here's how to use your fire extinguisher:

> P: Pull the pin.
> A: Aim at the base of the fire, staying at least six feet away.
> S: Squeeze the handle.
> S: Sweep the base of the fire from side to side.

Fire Safety

Outfit your home with several strategically placed smoke alarms.

A fire extinguisher should be ready and waiting near every high-risk area, with at least one available on each floor of your home.

Keep your back to the exit in case the fire spreads.

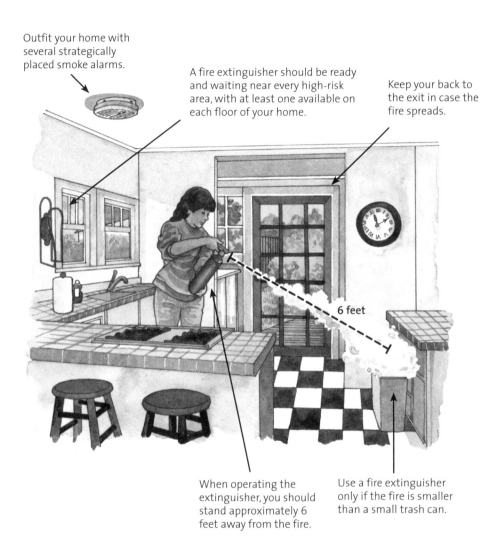

6 feet

When operating the extinguisher, you should stand approximately 6 feet away from the fire.

Use a fire extinguisher only if the fire is smaller than a small trash can.

With a baby in the house, it is more important than ever to pay attention to fire safety. In a fire, evacuate your child quickly and call 911. To be prepared for a smaller fire, equip your home with fire extinguishers. Practice safety drills and be prepared to use them properly in an emergency situation.

Replace when needed. Check your fire extinguisher's pressure gauge monthly. The pointer on the gauge must be in the green area. Have fire extinguishers serviced or checked according to the manufacturer's instructions. Get new fire extinguishers every fifteen years.

Get carbon monoxide alarms. Carbon monoxide (CO)—a clear, odorless, tasteless gas produced by malfunctioning fuel-burning appliances such as furnaces, gas dryers, ovens, and water heaters—can be deadly to small children, even in low levels. It kills more than 250 people in the United States each year. And babies are more vulnerable to it than adults.

CO alarms sound before CO levels grow to dangerous levels. Place a CO alarm outside every sleeping area and at least fifteen feet away from furnaces, wood stoves, fuel-burning kitchen stoves, and other fuel-burning appliances. Also place one near the door leading to the attached garage if you have one. (Though you should never leave a car running inside a garage.)

Choose battery-operated alarms, or at least ones with battery-backup, that will work even during a power outage.

Change the batteries. Just like with smoke alarms, make sure to swap out the batteries in your CO alarms at least once a year, such as when you change your clocks in October. And test the alarms once a month.

Know the symptoms of CO poisoning. Symptoms of CO poisoning include breathing difficulties, confusion, dizziness, headaches, fatigue, and nausea. If your CO alarm sounds, press the reset/silence button and get everyone out of the house or to an open window and call 911. Don't go back inside or move from the open window until the emergency services have arrived, the home is aired out, and the CO alarm doesn't reactivate.

Check for lead paint. The American Academy of Pediatrics says that even small amounts of lead can be harmful for children, contributing to problems such as aggressiveness, anemia, attention deficit, growth problems, learning disabilities, and lower IQs. Even though lead poisoning is one of the most preventable environmental health problems, nearly half a million children under age five in the United States have high lead levels in their blood.

The most common way for babies to be exposed to lead is by inhaling lead dust particles released from old paint. Children living in older homes are most at risk because lead was an ingredient in paint before 1977.

If you suspect your home has lead hazards, call the National Lead Information Center at 800-424-5323 for help.

Checking Window Coverings

If you're like millions of Americans, your windows are covered by window blinds. They're inexpensive, attractive, and functional. But what can you do to make sure they're safe?

First, move your baby's crib away from all windows. Preferably, put the crib against a wall without a window. Next, move any furniture that your child could climb on, such as a dresser, away from windows so your baby can't climb on the furniture to reach windows or the cords on blinds, pleated shades, or draperies. Do this in every room of your house, not just your baby's nursery.

If it's at all possible, replace corded window treatments in your baby's nursery and playroom with window treatments without cords (such as drapes or shades).

Next, take a look at the blinds in the rest of your home. How old are they? If your blinds were made after 2001, they include the latest safety measures. If your blinds were made before 2001, however, you should replace or retrofit them.

"There are millions of old window blinds and corded shades out there," says Michael Cienian, vice president of quality and engineering for Springs Window Fashions and president of the Window Covering Safety Council. "According to the U.S. Consumer Product Safety Commission, since 1990, there have been more than 200 reported cases of accidental child strangulations on corded window coverings."

Old blinds can be dangerous because their cords can form loops that can be strangulation hazards. This can be a problem with both the outer pull cords and the inner lift cords of blinds and shades.

The first concern is with the outer pull cord. If your blinds were made before 1995, the outer pull cords are likely in the form a loop. "If that's the case, cut the loop above the tassel, remove the tassel, and add a new safety tassel at the end of each cord," says Cienian. You can get new tassels for free from the Window Covering Safety Council at www.windowcoverings.org or 800-506-4636.

The second concern is with the inner lift cords. These are the cords that run between the window blind slats to raise and lower the blinds. If your blinds were made before 2001, a child can pull on the inner cords and potentially create a loop large enough to cause strangulation. Window blinds made since 2001 have attachments on the pull cords so the inner lift cords can't loop. You can get free cord-stops to retrofit pre-2001 blinds and shades from the Window Covering Safety Council.

Even if you have the newest window blinds, it's important to always lock the blind into position, including when it comes to rest on the windowsill. (This eliminates the possibility of a loop forming.) Cut the pull cords as short as you can and keep them out of your child's reach.

Some window treatments, such as vertical blinds and traverse draperies, have pull cords that require a continuous loop to operate and can't be cut. "Permanently anchor them to the floor or wall with tie-downs," Cienian says. Vertical blinds and draperies manufactured after 1997 are equipped with attached tie-downs. Free retrofit tie-downs are also available from the council.

As mentioned previously, to attempt to completely eliminate any possible danger from window cords, consider replacing your blinds with cordless window coverings, especially in children's bedrooms and playrooms. Cordless blinds, for example, use spring-loaded mechanisms, battery- or motor-operated lift controls, or simple wand pulls instead of cords. Cordless shades or curtains are another alternative. And, according to Cienian, "Cordless blinds are more common and more affordable now."

WINDOW TREATMENT SAFETY

When window cords are within reach, young children may become entangled and accidentally strangle. Check your window treatments for potential hazards, and if necessary change them out or retrofit them with the modern recommended safety features.

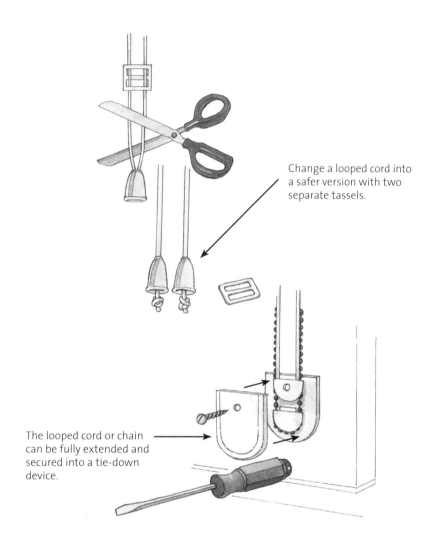

Change a looped cord into a safer version with two separate tassels.

The looped cord or chain can be fully extended and secured into a tie-down device.

Eliminating looped pull cords, installing cords stops, and retrofitting looped cord blinds with inexpensive tie-down devices are all smart ways to make your existing window treatments safer. When purchasing new blinds, consider the safer cordless styles.

Deal with lead paint. Lead was banned from house paint in 1978. However, it could still be present in older homes. If there is lead paint in your home, either have a licensed professional remove it completely or cover it with an approved sealant. Until then, wash your child's hands and face, as well as his toys, often to reduce his exposure to lead-contaminated dust.

Keep it covered. If you've painted over lead paint, check regularly for peeling and chipping.

Keep clean. Control the amount of lead dust in your home by mopping floors and sponging walls and surfaces weekly, using an all-purpose household cleaner. Clean carpets with a high-efficiency particulate air (HEPA) vacuum.

Run the water. If your home has lead pipes, run the tap water for a minute before using it for drinking or cooking. Use cold water for mixing formula, drinking, or cooking because hot water contains higher levels of lead.

Replace old blinds and vinyl flooring. Old vinyl mini-blinds and old vinyl flooring can release lead dust. Replace them. For more information on lead poisoning, visit www.epa.gov/lead.

Light the way. Place nightlights at key locations to light up the path from your bedroom to the nursery and bathroom.

Check the banisters. Make sure that you have strong banisters along each stairway of your home. You'll be carrying your baby up and down the stairs, so you need sturdy banisters to hold onto.

Keep your home clutter free. Make a policy to keep walkways, and especially staircases, clutter free. When you're walking around carrying your baby, you don't want to trip.

Fasten down rugs. Make sure any throw rugs are fastened down. Or get rid of them entirely. They can be tripping hazards.

Clean up. Get into the habit of cleaning up spills, such as water or oil in the kitchen, right away to prevent falls.

Checking Your Water

In addition to lead, your water could also be contaminated with bacteria, copper, and other heavy metals, nitrates, pesticides, and viruses. If you have public or municipal water, call your water supplier, which must test its water regularly. If you ask, they might test your home's water for free to see whether any contaminants are getting into the water between the plant and you. If they won't test the water—or if you use well water—you can have it tested at a state-certified lab. Call the Environmental Protection Agency's Safe Drinking Water hotline at 800-426-4791 to find a lab. The whole battery of tests costs around $200.

Surprisingly, lead can be a concern in almost any home's water. Lead pipes and copper pipes with lead solder are common in older homes. Lead solder was legally used to join pipes until 1986. Even today, faucets are allowed to contain as much as 8 percent lead, and they can leach a significant amount of lead into the water. Plus if you have copper pipes, some of that copper could be leaching into your water.

Installing Ground Fault Circuit Interrupters

Install ground fault circuit interrupters (GFCIs) on outlets near water. These gadgets stop the electrical current when an appliance gets wet. You should have them on outlets in rooms with water, such as the bathroom, kitchen, and laundry room.

Watch out for VOCs. Chemicals found in many common products, called volatile organic compounds or VOCs, could raise your baby's risk of developing asthma, according to an Australian study. The researchers found that of eighty-eight children who were treated for asthma at an emergency room, those who were exposed to higher levels of VOCs were four times more likely to develop asthma than the children exposed to lower levels.

VOCs are emitted from products such as air fresheners, cleaning products, floor adhesives, new carpet, and paints. When you're using these products, keep your baby away and open doors and windows for ventilation. Also consider using less-toxic cleaning alternatives, such as vinegar and baking soda.

Reduce chemical use. Experts don't know for sure how household toxins—such as pesticides, paints, and cleaning products—affect babies, but they are much more vulnerable because they weigh less than adults, they are closer to the ground where toxic vapors and dust accumulate, and they put their hands, which pick up toxins, into their mouths.

Try to get rid of pests without chemicals, for example by sealing and caulking cracks in walls. Pregnant women shouldn't use pesticides at all. Always leave windows open when using paints and stains. And switch to less-toxic cleaning products, such as Simple Green cleanser and Seventh Generation laundry soap.

Just say no. If anyone in your home smokes, now is the time to quit. Babies exposed to tobacco during pregnancy are two to three times more likely to die of Sudden Infant Death Syndrome (SIDS). Secondhand smoke puts your baby at risk for SIDS also. Each year, nearly 15,000 babies under eighteen months old are hospitalized because of respiratory infections linked to secondhand smoke. Exposure to secondhand smoke also increases middle-ear infections.

Safety Alert: Checking for Mold

A new study found that children under age two raised in homes with a moldy smell are twice as likely to develop asthma by age seven. Mold produces allergens, irritants, and possibly even toxins. If you smell or see mold, it's important to get rid of it. Here's how:

- Fix any leaks.
- Reduce moisture with a dehumidifier.
- Clean moldy floors and walls with detergent or bleach, using rubber gloves and an N-95 mask, which are sold at hardware stores.
- Consider hiring a professional with mold removal experience if the moldy area is more than three feet square.

Cigarette smoke contains more than 2,000 chemicals, and fifty of them are known to be cancer causing. A recent study found cancer-causing chemicals in urine samples from nearly half of the infants of parents who smoked. Scientists are concerned that these children may be more susceptible to lung cancer once they reach adulthood. Yet 40 percent of kids under age five live with a smoker. Commit to keeping your baby's environment smoke free.

Even thirdhand smoke—the smoke that you can smell that's seeped into clothing, furniture, or car upholstery—is dangerous. It contains chemicals that are re-released into the air for your baby to inhale, which seem to have the same effect as a low dose of secondhand smoke.

Safety Alert: Looking for the UL Label

Make sure that products that you use and new products that you buy bear the Underwriters Laboratories (UL) label, says John Drengenberg, an electrical engineer and consumer affairs manager for UL, a nonprofit product safety certification organization. Those labels are everywhere—the letters "UL" in a circle. But what do they mean? For more than 100 years, UL has tested products to make sure they meet applicable safety requirements. It tests products in more than 19,000 categories—everything from hair driers to roof shingles to outlet covers to televisions. It conducts more than 100,000 investigations each year, and each product undergoes dozens of tests, checking for hazards such as fire, electrical hazards, mechanical problems, sharp edges, and even radiation.

For example, UL tests to make sure that the glass front of your oven doesn't get so hot that it burns your toddler when he touches it. It checks to make sure that the beam of the laser in the supermarket checkout scanner isn't so focused that it harms your child's eyes if he looks into it. And it ensures that if you drop your hair dryer onto the tile bathroom floor it won't crack so that your toddler could stick his finger into it and get shocked.

And then, once products have been approved, manufacturers must agree that UL can drop into their factories unannounced, at any time, to ensure that the products still meet UL requirements.

Manufacturers don't have to submit their products for UL testing; it's voluntary. However, large retailers in the United States won't sell products that haven't been UL tested. So as you might imagine, most manufacturers submit their products for testing. In fact, in many categories of consumer products, such as appliances, electronics, and television sets, nearly 100 percent of the products are UL tested.

Watch out for deep discount retailers and street vendors, though. That's where you're most likely to find products sold that haven't been UL tested and certified. Also watch out for garage sales. If you buy a product there, make sure it has a UL label. If it doesn't, perhaps the owner removed it. But perhaps it was never there. You have no way to know for sure.

Read product instruction manuals. They contain critical information that, along with the rigorous testing that UL puts products through, helps to protect consumers.

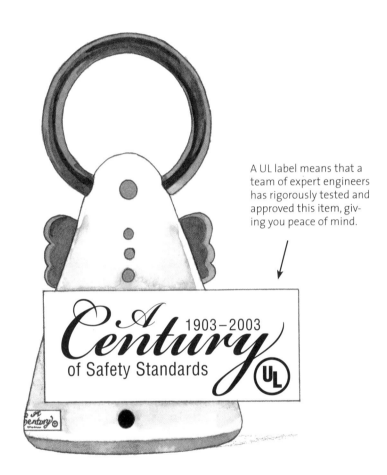

A UL label means that a team of expert engineers has rigorously tested and approved this item, giving you peace of mind.

Look for the Underwriters Laboratories label on products you use and especially on any new items you plan to purchase—not just items for your baby, but also on appliances and gadgets all over your home.

Safety Alert: Preparing Your Dog or Cat for Your Baby

Your pet probably already senses that big changes are afoot. Here's how to ease the transition for him:

- During your pregnancy, prepare a comfortable, special area for your pet inside your house, such as a dog crate or a cat bed. This will provide a safe retreat for him once the baby arrives.

- Get your pet used to the sounds of a baby by playing recordings of baby noises. You can make one yourself with the help of another baby, or you can buy one such as "Preparing Fido," a collection of baby sounds, which is available at www.preparingfido.com or 800-953-5211.

- Desensitize your pet to the rough handling of young children. At least five minutes a day for two to five minutes, touch him between his paw pads; on his face, tail, and belly; and in his ears and mouth. Start gently. If the dog resists, have someone else give him treats while you do the touching.

- Walk your dog with your new stroller and while you're wearing your baby carrier to get him used to them.

- Continue to give your pet all of the attention and treats he's used to so he knows he's still an important member of the family.

- If there will be times that both your baby and your pet will need to ride together in your car, prepare for that now. You'll need a way to keep them safe and separate, such as by confining the pet to a crate or to a specific area with a barrier.

- Simulate baby-feeding time either in your bed or nursing chair. Give your pet a toy or treat and encourage him to go to his safe retreat place.

- Set up the baby's nursery early so that your pet can get used to having the new furniture and baby gear around.

- Train your cat to stay out of the baby's crib by putting aluminum foil on the mattress before you bring the baby home. Cats don't like the sound and feel of the foil, so after one try, they'll stay out.

- Install a sturdy gate to keep your pet out of the nursery when unsupervised.
- Use baby products on yourself so your pet gets used to the scent.
- If a new person will be helping you to watch and care for the pet after your baby arrives, introduce him or her to your pet now.
- Come up with a plan for caring for your pet while you're having the baby. Make sure the caregiver has access to your home and has all of the instructions he or she will need.
- Make sure that your pet is up to date on vaccines and has been checked for parasites.
- Keep your cat indoors to minimize exposure to fleas and ticks. This keeps your cat safer as well.
- While you're pregnant, another reason to keep your cat indoors is so he can't hunt small animals, which can transmit toxoplasmosis, a disease that may increase the risk of miscarriage or fetal deformities. Avoid stray or outdoor cats. Have your partner clean the litter box daily. If you have to do it yourself, wear rubber gloves and wash both your hands and the gloves thoroughly when you're finished.
- If you haven't done so already, consider having your pet spayed or neutered, which may decrease aggression.
- As long as your pet doesn't have a history of biting, let him interact with children during your pregnancy. If the dog growls or cat hisses, seek professional training.
- Address any behavior problems now. Enroll your dog in an obedience class or see an animal-behavior specialist. You can do this when a puppy is as young as twelve weeks. Especially consider this if the pet starts behaving drastically different while you're pregnant.
- Consider taking a baby-readiness class, which is offered by some trainers and vets. They prepare dogs for living with young children, perform a temperament test to see how well your pet will do around children, and give lots of advice on how to help everyone get along.

PART II

Birth to Six Months

So precious, so tiny. Your baby at this age pretty much stays in one spot. But still there are home-safety precautions you should take, beginning on day one.

Your baby is most fragile in his first four months. His head is bigger than his body, and his neck isn't strong enough to stabilize it. A newborn's bones are very delicate, and squeezing too tightly can cause fractures.

Yet your baby grows stronger every day. Sometime between birth and three months, your baby will start to raise his head, and soon his shoulders and chest, to explore the world around him. He's learning how to coordinate his limbs.

Around four months, your babyproofing job will become a lot more challenging. That's when your baby will figure out that the best way to learn about a new object is to put it into his mouth. And by that time, he'll be coordinated enough to get things such as the TV remote control, the dog's tennis ball, and your slippers into his mouth. Ick.

Around six months, your baby may start putting even more things into his mouth, but for a different reason. When your baby starts teething, chewing on hard objects might soothe his sore gums.

Around four to six months, your baby will have greater trunk strength and equilibrium. He'll learn how to roll over and later sit up. Once he figures out how to sit up well and crawl, move on to the babyproofing tips in Part III.

The Nursery

Where your baby sleeps is a very personal decision. Some parents firmly believe a baby should sleep in her crib from day one, while others prefer to have a family bed. Still other parents strike a compromise, having their babies sleep in cradles or bassinets in their rooms. Here's how to make your baby's nursery safe.

Safety Alert: Sleeping Hazards

Sleeping like a baby; it sounds so blissful. Yet it's a terrible fact that each year approximately 2,000 babies go to sleep and don't wake up, making Sudden Infant Death Syndrome (SIDS) the number one cause of death for babies from one month to one year old. SIDS risk peaks from two to four months and is minimal after six months. Here's how to keep your sleeping baby safe:

- According to First Candle, a group that fights SIDS, the safest sleeping place for a baby is a separate area (such as a crib or bassinet) next to the adult bed for at least the first six months.

  According to a recent study by the U.S. Consumer Product Safety Commission, the risk of suffocation in babies under eleven months who sleep in adult beds rather than cribs is forty times higher. It's especially important not to put your baby to sleep in your bed if you are overly tired, on medication, or under the effects of drugs or alcohol because you'll be less likely to wake up if you roll over onto the baby.

- If you decide to co-sleep, make sure your mattress fits tightly against the headboard and footboard and remove pillows, comforters, and thick blankets from your bed.

- Don't let infants and toddlers sleep next to each other. They sleep so soundly that a toddler might not wake up if she rolls over onto the baby.

- Always put your baby to sleep on her back. Be sure that your baby's caregivers know this as well. People of previous generations were taught to put babies to sleep on their stomachs.

  "It's especially important for babies who are used to sleeping on their backs to be placed on their backs. If these babies are placed to sleep on their stomachs, their risk of SIDS goes up twenty times," says Bill Schmid, founder and vice president of research and development for Halo Innovations.

  Since the national Back to Sleep campaign began in 1994, the SIDS rate in the United States has decreased by more than 50 percent, the equivalent of sparing the lives of more than 3,500 babies each year.

Safety Alert: Sleeping Hazards (continued)

- Avoid side sleeping. It's been shown to be more dangerous than back sleeping.

- If your baby has a medical problem that calls for her to sleep on her stomach—such as a birth defect, frequent spitting up after eating, or a breathing, lung, or heart problem—talk with her pediatrician about the best sleep position for her.

- Place your baby on a firm mattress, and never on a soft mattress, sofa, sofa cushion, waterbed, sheep skin, or another soft surface.

- Keep pillows, quilts, soft toys, and other soft items out of the crib. Though they might look adorable, they can pose suffocation hazards.

- Never put your baby down on a mattress covered with plastic or a plastic bag.

- Encourage your baby to use a pacifier for sleep for the first year. (If your baby is breastfed, wait until she's one month old to introduce a pacifier to ensure that breastfeeding is firmly established.) Using a pacifier has been shown to reduce the risk of SIDS. Experts think that a pacifier increases a baby's sensitivity to stimuli, making her more likely to wake if she gets into a position that interferes with breathing.

- Instead of placing a blanket over your baby, dress her in a one-piece bunting. Other options include zippered sleep sacks and swaddling blankets that stay in place with Velcro. If you insist on a blanket, place your baby's feet at the bottom of the crib (think "feet to foot"), keep the blanket at waist height, and tuck the ends firmly under the sides and bottom of the mattress.

- Keep your baby's room warm, but not too warm. Aim for a room temperature between 68°F and 72°F (20°C and 22°C). According to Schmid, that's the temperature most people feel comfortable in short sleeves. Continue to monitor your baby for clues that she's comfortable.

- Never put an electric blanket or heating pad in a crib.

SAFE SLEEPING

Make sure the mattress is firm and the crib is free of objects.

Your baby should always be put to sleep on her back; the use of a "wedge" to keep from rolling over is not recommended.

Studies show using a pacifier reduces the risk of SIDS.

For warmth and coziness, a one-piece bunting is preferable to a blanket, which can shift, bunch up, and impede your baby's breathing.

Always put your baby to sleep on her back. Back sleepers are twenty times less likely to succumb to SIDS, which is the leading cause of death among infants one month to one year old.

Don't use sleep positioners. These wedge-shaped pieces of foam are designed to keep infants on their backs. But experts think they can be suffocation hazards. And there is no proof that they lower the risk of SIDS.

Don't swaddle your baby with loose blankets. "Nurses in hospitals are very good at swaddling babies in blankets so that they don't come off, but it must be done properly and with the right size blanket. Most parents aren't able to do this, and the baby breaks out and has a loose blanket in his crib," says Bill Schmid, founder and vice president of research and development of Halo Innovations. A new product called the SleepSack Swaddle incorporates a swaddle into a SleepSack wearable blanket, so the baby is less likely to wriggle out of it. Once the baby outgrows the swaddler, you can remove it and just use the SleepSack alone.

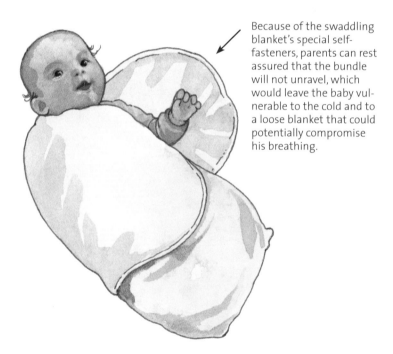

Because of the swaddling blanket's special self-fasteners, parents can rest assured that the bundle will not unravel, which would leave the baby vulnerable to the cold and to a loose blanket that could potentially compromise his breathing.

Recent research shows that swaddling can help reduce the risk of SIDS by promoting better sleep when infants are on their backs. Innovative products such as swaddle blankets make it easy for a new parent to bundle the baby up expertly and safely.

Safety Supplies: Halo SleepSack Wearable Blanket

First Candle warns against covering your baby with, or swaddling your baby in, a blanket. A blanket can cover your baby's nose or mouth and cause her to re-breathe her own carbon dioxide. Instead, to keep your baby warm and safe in her crib, First Candle recommends putting her in a wearable blanket. These sleeveless sacks zip up the front, so they're easy to put on your baby. They're made of soft, flame-resistant cotton or fleece, and they offer plenty of room for your baby to kick her feet. The blankets are sleeveless so that bulky sleeves can't interfere with your baby's breathing or cause your baby to overheat.

Each blanket has "Back to Sleep" embroidered on its chest, as a reminder to parents and caregivers to always place babies on their backs to sleep. Another safety feature of a wearable blanket is that it keeps a baby from kicking her feet enough to roll over onto her stomach.

Check the rails. Always lock the side rail in its raised position when your baby is in her crib.

Never tie anything around a baby's neck. This includes pacifiers, necklaces, and headbands. Also remove your baby's bib before you place her in her crib or play yard.

Zip tight. Make sure your baby's pajamas fasten with zippers instead of snaps. "Snaps are more likely to come off and become choking hazards," says Schmid.

Buy flame-retardant sleepwear. It should be either polyester or treated cotton. Also, sleepwear should fit snugly. Snug-fitting sleepwear is less likely to catch on fire and won't burn as rapidly because there's less air between the clothing and the skin.

Cotton sweatshirts and pants that aren't labeled as sleepwear generally aren't flame-retardant. Avoid these and other loose-fitting sleepwear. Clothes that aren't flame-retardant should be labeled with a yellow tag that indicates they should fit snugly for safety.

Safety Alert: Shaken Baby Syndrome

Never shake a baby.

When a baby is held by her arms, or under her arms, and shaken, her brain bounces violently back and forth against the inside of her skull. The force of that impact can damage the retinas of her eyes and tear open the veins that attach her brain to the inside of her head. Blood can pool inside her skull. Brain cells swell and die. All of this trauma can cause the baby to stop breathing, which causes oxygen deprivation and leads to further brain damage. It happens in just 5 to 15 seconds.

This is called Shaken Baby Syndrome (SBS). It happens to approximately 1,300 babies each year, 1,200 of whom are under a year old. Babies are far less able to hold their heads steady, and their brains are softer and more easily injured than adults. But anyone—toddler, child, teen, or adult—who is shaken hard enough can be injured or killed.

SBS is most often triggered by frustration over incessant crying. Anyone can snap, and to a person already under stress, and likely sleep deprived, an infant's inconsolable crying is especially nerve-jangling.

You must maintain control. Here are some strategies that work:

- Understand that it's normal for babies to cry, even when all of their needs have been met.
- Take a break. Ask a friend to come help and get away. If no one is available to help, place your baby in her crib, close the door, and leave the room for a few minutes.
- Get some exercise. Take your baby out for a walk or put her in a swing and do an exercise video.
- Turn on soothing music.

If you even suspect that your baby has been shaken, take her to the emergency room right away. Treatments and therapy can help dramatically in some cases.

Inspect the pacifier. If you notice a change in your baby's pacifier, such as a tear or holes, discard it. Pacifiers can deteriorate from age and exposure to sunlight.

Move the mobile. When your baby is five months old or beginning to push up on her hands and knees, whichever comes first, remove any mobiles and toys strung across her crib.

"Instead of using a mobile, which you have to remove from your baby's crib when she's able to sit up, paint a mural on the ceiling," says Shalena Smith, owner of Ga Ga Designs, a Los Angeles–based interior design company that specializes in nurseries and kids' rooms. "This gives your baby something to look at, and it has the added benefit of being art that can't fall down on her. Be sure to use nontoxic, water-based paint."

Supervise sleep. If you allow your baby to sleep in a bouncer seat or infant carrier (which some experts advise against), supervise her. Because a baby doesn't have good head control, her head could fall forward, making it difficult for her to breathe.

Keep supplies close. Place diaper-changing supplies—diapers, wipes, diaper rash cream, a diaper pail—within reach of the changing table. In the split second you turn away to toss out a dirty diaper, your baby could roll over and fall to the floor.

However, keep toiletries out of your baby's reach. Baby oil, for instance, can get into a baby's lungs and be very dangerous.

Hang on. Usually, newborns stay put during diaper changes, but keep a hand on your baby at all times in case she gets a burst of energy and rolls. And when your baby learns how to roll over, which could be around four months, she'll want to show those new skills off.

Use the safety strap. Always use the safety strap on your changing table. But even with the strap, never leave your baby unattended.

"Use the safety features of your baby products all of the time, such as the safety strap on your baby's changing table," says Amy Chezem, Juvenile Product Manufacturers Association communications director. "But keep in mind that these safety features aren't a replacement for your own eyes watching your baby."

My Safety Story

Never underestimate what your child can do. One day I was changing my four-month-old baby, who had not yet learned to roll over. The diapers were across the room from the changing table, and no one else was home to get one for me. When I stepped away from the changing table to get a diaper, I heard the plop. It was the first time my daughter rolled over, and she rolled right off the changing table onto the floor. Thankfully, the floor was carpeted, and the only result was that it scared us both. It doesn't matter if your baby is one month old or fourteen years old, she will always surprise you by what she can do!

—Bryan Burke, M.D., general pediatrician and associate professor at the University of Arkansas for Medical Sciences and Arkansas Children's Hospital

Place a rug under your baby's changing table. This will provide a bit of cushioning in case of a fall.

Use the floor. If you're worried your baby might fall off of her changing table, change her diaper on the floor, using a receiving blanket as a changing pad.

Wash up. Always wash your hands after changing your baby's diaper.

Consider pop-ups. Pop-up baby wipes, while more expensive than regular wipes, are easy to grab with one hand. That way you can keep your other hand on your baby at all times.

Buy the right powder. Don't buy baby powder that contains talc. It can harm your baby's lungs if she inhales it. Try cornstarch instead.

Go cool. If you use a humidifier or vaporizer, use a cool-mist one, not a hot-steam one.

Post a sign. Hang a dry erase board on the outside of your baby's nursery. Record information for your spouse or other caregiver, such as when you gave the baby a dose of medicine or when she went down for a nap.

Stay in the home. Never leave your baby at home alone, even for a moment while you go for the mail or to move the car. It takes only seconds for a fire to blaze or an accident to happen.

CHANGING TABLE SAFETY

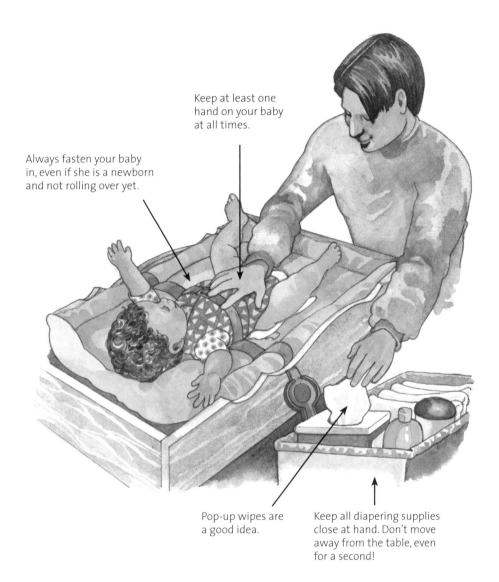

Keep at least one hand on your baby at all times.

Always fasten your baby in, even if she is a newborn and not rolling over yet.

Pop-up wipes are a good idea.

Keep all diapering supplies close at hand. Don't move away from the table, even for a second!

Changing table safety features provide us some peace of mind. But there is no replacement for a vigilant parent. Your baby might roll over at any time, so don't take chances by relying on the safety strap and walking away.

The Kitchen

With a new baby in the house, you might be on a first-name basis with the pizza delivery person, but you will have to go into the kitchen sometime. And when you do, it's critical to keep safety in mind.

Prevent scalds and burns. Never drink or carry hot beverages or foods while holding or carrying your baby. And keep them out of your baby's reach.

"Some of the worst burns I've seen are from coffee," says Garry Gardner, M.D., a pediatrician in private practice in Darien, Illinois, and former member of the American Academy of Pediatrics Committee on Injury, Violence, and Poison Prevention. "Coffee seeps right through clothing and almost instantly causes third-degree burns."

Be aware. Whenever you're carrying hot food or beverages, know exactly where your baby is so you don't trip over him or spill the food or drink on him.

Set right. When getting ready for meals, place hot foods and beverages near the center of the table to prevent them from spilling onto your baby. Or serve hot food from the stove or countertop instead of the table.

Take extra care around the stove. Get into the habit of using the back burners on your stove and turn pot handles toward the back of the stove.

Never hold your baby while you're cooking. Instead put your baby in a safe place so you can keep an eye on what you're cooking. Unattended cooking is the number one cause of cooking fires.

Keep your stove top and countertops clean and uncluttered, and keep curtains and other flammable items far away.

Soothe sore gums. When your baby starts teething, he's likely to pick up anything and everything to chew on it in an effort to ease the pain. Divert his attention from the plastic soda bottle, for example, to a cold teething ring. (But be sure to follow the manufacturer's instructions first: Most say to cool teethers in the refrigerator only, not in the freezer.)

Safety Supplies: Stove Guards

Splatter guards attach to the front of your stove and keep hot liquids from splashing onto your baby. They also prevent him from reaching up and touching the burners. (Though ideally he won't be close enough to the stove for that to happen anyway.) They cost around $23 through baby safety supplies catalogs.

KITCHEN SAFETY

Keep your baby at a safe distance.

Rotate handles away from the front of the stove.

Get in the habit of using out-of-reach rear burners.

Splatter guards protect your baby from scalding spills and splatters.

Now is the time to get in the habit of keeping your kitchen safe. Your baby will soon be an inquisitive toddler and you'll want to be ready!

Safety Alert: Feeding

Feeding a baby is an absolute delight. Here's how to make sure it's safe, too:

- For your baby's first four weeks, sterilize his bottles, bottle nipples, and all breast pump parts. Here's how: Boil the items in water for 10 minutes or wash them in the dishwasher. Use a sterile cotton swab to clean nooks and crannies.
- Before feeding your baby, wash your hands with soap and warm water for ten seconds. Dry them with a paper towel.
- Choose a comfortable place where you will both be safe and relaxed.
- If you're mixing formula, regular tap water is fine to use for most healthy babies. But ask your baby's pediatrician if you should boil it first to kill bacteria. If you boil it, do so for only one minute. Longer can concentrate harmful substances such as nitrates.
- If there's a chance your home's pipes have lead, always use cold water to make formula and let the water run for 1 minute first.
- If you use bottled water to make formula and it doesn't contain fluoride, ask your baby's pediatrician if your baby needs fluoride supplements.
- Don't warm baby bottles in the microwave. The liquid may heat unevenly, resulting in hot spots that can scald your baby's mouth. And if you're using breast milk, microwaving or boiling can destroy valuable immunological components.
- Watch out for "expiration dates" on breast milk. Here's how long it keeps:
    - Frozen in a deep freezer at 0°F (18°C): six months or longer
    - Frozen in a freezer/refrigerator combo: three to four months
    - Frozen in a freezer compartment within the fridge: two months

Safety Alert: Feeding (continued)

- Check expiration dates on formula; each can should have a "use by" date.

- Don't use dented formula cans. If the inside tin layer is cracked, the liquid may come in contact with the steel, potentially causing rust.

- Store unopened formula in a cool, dry place.

- Wash the top of the formula can before opening it.

- When preparing formula, follow the manufacturer's instructions carefully, using a standard measuring cup instead of the lines on your baby's bottle. Adding too little water can tax your baby's kidneys and cause dehydration, while adding too much water will deprive your baby of the calories and nutrients she needs.

- If your baby doesn't finish his bottle within one hour, discard the remainder. Bacteria from his mouth can seep into the bottle, contaminate its contents, and make him sick if he drinks it later.

- If you take pumped breast milk or formula to go, pack it in an insulated bag with an ice pack.

- Once you prepare formula, follow the manufacturer's directions for storage. You can usually store it covered in the refrigerator for twenty-four hours.

- Never buy or borrow a used breast pump. Pumps are like tooth-brushes; every new mother needs her own. Bacteria and viruses can cling to a pump's internal diaphragm, which can't be removed, replaced, or fully sterilized. Research suggests that bacteria and viruses can be transmitted through breast milk. The only exception to this rule is hospital-grade rental pumps. They have special barriers that prevent cross-contamination, and they are designed for multiple users.

- Choose the best type of breast pump for you. Hospital-grade pumps are fast and efficient, but noisy and heavy. Professional, midweight pumps are quick, but costly. Small electric or battery-operated pumps are portable and inexpensive, but slow. Manual pumps are the least expensive option, but they can cause repeti-tive strain injuries if you use them frequently.

- Wash any parts of the breast pump that touch your breasts or milk in the dishwasher or with hot, soapy water and allow them to air dry. (Follow the manufacturer's instructions.)

- Thoroughly wash and dry all bottles, bottle nipples, and breast-pump parts before putting them away.

- Discard any bottle nipples that appear cracked or stained.

The Bathroom

Those first ventures into the bathroom to give your new baby a bath are bound to be an adventure for both of you.

"Be extra careful with children in bathrooms," says Garry Gardner, M.D., a pediatrician in private practice in Darien, Illinois, and former member of the American Academy of Pediatrics Committee on Injury, Violence, and Poison Prevention. "The bathroom is a room where parents are often distracted, but you must always keep your antenna up."

Get a mat. Put nonslip mats in the bathtub and on the floor next to the tub. This is to ensure you don't slip in the bathroom on a wet floor while carrying your baby.

Trim with care. A baby's fingernails grow surprisingly fast and need to be cut as often as twice a week. Toenails grow more slowly, and they don't need to be as short as fingernails, so they usually need to be cut only once a month. To avoid cutting your baby's skin along with her nails, hold her finger firmly and press the finger pad away from the nail as you cut. Use a nail-care kit designed for babies, with small clippers and rounded scissors.

Trim your baby's nails right after a bath, when they're softer. Or trim them when she's asleep in her car seat or stroller. Trim her fingernails on a curve to prevent sharp edges and clip her toenails straight across to prevent ingrown nails.

Skip the bandages. If you cut your baby's skin while clipping her nails, don't put a bandage on it. It could come off and become a choking hazard if she gets her finger into her mouth.

Keep away. Don't allow your baby nearby when hot appliances such as curling irons are plugged in and turned on. Even an infant might be able to grab a cord and pull the appliance down onto herself. According to the U.S. Consumer Product Safety Commission, 7,700 children each year are treated in emergency rooms after burning themselves on hot curling irons.

Check the plug. Make sure your hair dryer has a large, rectangular plug, says John Drengenberg, an electrical engineer and consumer affairs manager for Underwriters Laboratories (UL), a nonprofit product safety certification organization. If a plugged-in electrical appliance, such as a hair dryer, falls into water, even if it is turned off, someone touching that water could be electrocuted. The human body is a much better conductor of electricity than water, so the electricity shoots through the body. However, inside those special hair dryer plugs is a circuit that senses the water and in milliseconds, shuts off the power, keeping you safe.

Check the dose. Many infant medication dosages are based on age. But if your baby is big for her age, she might not get enough medication, and if she's small for her age, she might get too much. Check with your baby's pediatrician for weight-specific dosages.

Turn on a light. Never give your baby medication in the dark. Without seeing what you're doing, you might give the wrong dosage or even the wrong drug.

Safety Alert: Bathing

Between two and eight weeks, after your baby's umbilical cord stump has fallen off, it's time to give her a bath. This is a great bonding activity, and most babies love it.

But please be safe. Each year more than fifty babies under age one drown. According to Safe Kids USA, more than half of infant drownings occur in bathtubs. A baby can drown in a very small amount of water—the amount that covers her nose and mouth. Even an inch. Never leave your baby alone in—or near— any amount of water, for even a second. Here's how to bathe your baby safely:

- If you're using an infant tub, you can use it almost anywhere—in the kitchen or bathroom sink, on the changing table, or inside the big tub. Or you could simply bathe your baby in the sink, with the faucet turned away and soft towels or a foam insert in the bottom.

- Gather all of your supplies—soap, washcloth, towel, temperature gauge, fresh diaper, and clean clothes—by the tub before you put your baby in. Choose a mild bath soap, one with a neutral pH and minimal dyes and fragrances. A hooded towel is especially helpful to wrap your baby in after her bath.

- Always turn the cold water on first and turn it off last when running water in the sink or bathtub.

- Add only enough water to the tub to cover your baby's legs—2 to 3 inches (5 to 7 cm).

- Check the temperature of the bath water with your wrist or elbow before putting your baby into it. (Your fingers and palms are not as sensitive to temperature.) The water should be warm, not hot— between 96°F and 100°F (35.5°C and 38°C). This is important for safety, but also because babies and toddlers generally prefer a much cooler tub than adults.

- To adjust the temperature, add hot water to cold, never the other way around.
- Turn off the water before putting your baby in. While the water is still running, the water temperature could change.• Turn off the faucets tightly so the water can't drip on your baby.
- Swirl the water with your hand to make sure there are no hot spots.
- If you're worried your baby might slip out of your hands, wear a pair of white cotton gloves and place a terry cloth towel on the bottom of the tub.
- Lift your baby gently into the bath, supporting her head, neck, and back on your arm while curling your fingers around her outer arm (kind of like how you'd cradle a football). This leaves your other hand free to wash your baby.
- As you bathe your baby, keep one hand under her armpit to keep her head out of the water.
- Hold your baby securely and wash her quickly if she's upset.
- Wash your baby's body before her hair to keep her from getting chilled.
- Whenever a baby is in the bath, an adult must be within arm's length, providing touch supervision, and not distracted by talking on the telephone or with another person or doing chores. Never leave a baby unsupervised in the tub for even a second. If you must leave the tubside for a phone call or to answer the door, wrap your baby in a towel and take her with you. Never rely on another child to supervise a baby in a bathtub.

BATHING

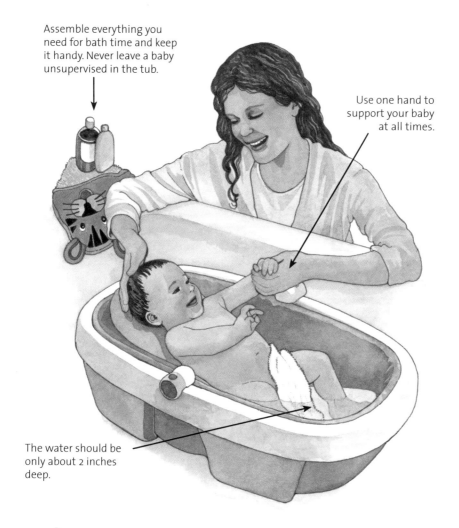

Assemble everything you need for bath time and keep it handy. Never leave a baby unsupervised in the tub.

Use one hand to support your baby at all times.

The water should be only about 2 inches deep.

Even an inch of water can be fatal to a baby, so never leave your child alone in any amount of water, for even a second.

Safety Supplies: Bath Pal Thermometers

These toys float on the water and change color if the bath water gets too warm to be safe for your baby. Some of them have a baby-pleasing duck or seal on top. They cost around $3 at baby supplies stores and major retailers.

Safety Supplies: Tubside Kneeler and Step Stools

Kneeling next to the tub to bathe your baby can be a real pain in the back. Yet for safety's sake, you can't leave that tubside while your baby is in the bath. The Tubside Kneeler and Step Stool has a padded surface to kneel on, and it comes with an attachable soft elbow cushion and accessory bag. When your child is old enough to use the sink herself, turn the cushion over to create a stable stool. They cost around $15 at major retailers.

The Living Room

We call them "living rooms" for a reason: We all spend lots of time there. Here's how to make your baby's living room time safe.

Be firm. A lot of parents place babies in their play yards to sleep (which some experts caution against). Don't add bedding or mattresses to the play yard. It's important to follow the same safe sleeping precautions for a play yard as for a crib. Keep pillows, quilts, comforters, and extra mattresses out. Soft bedding can become molded around a baby's face and suffocate him. Your baby should always sleep on his back on a firm, flat mattress.

Stick up. Put the play yard sides up. If the sides aren't locked in place, the play yard could collapse or the baby could roll into the space between the mattress and loose mesh sides and suffocate.

Nap solo. It's best to place your baby in his crib to nap. Research has shown it's particularly hazardous for babies to sleep on a couch with an adult. So be careful not to doze off in front of the TV while holding your baby.

Handle with care. Help friends and relatives who may be unfamiliar holding a baby handle yours gently. Teach them to support his head a little higher than his body, with the crook of their elbow or hand.

Buckle up. Always strap your baby into his swing; don't rely on the tray. Similarly, even before your baby is able to roll over, always strap your baby into his bouncer seat.

Swing alone. Don't put soft things such as blankets and stuffed animals in the swing with your baby. They could suffocate him.

Safety Supplies: Cradle Me Receiving Blanket

When other people are holding your baby, it's natural to worry about whether they're supporting his head correctly. The Cradle Me Receiving Blanket is a receiving blanket with a removable foam insert that provides neck support. You swaddle your baby in the Cradle Me just as you would any receiving blanket. They cost around $30 at online retailers and children's clothing stores. Search www.babyboo.com to find one near you.

Don't leave your baby alone. Get into the habit now of never leaving your baby alone anywhere, even for a moment, where he might fall. Even if he isn't rolling now, tiny babies can kick, push, roll, and scoot themselves off of beds and sofas, out of bouncer seats, and off of changing tables. Plus babies learn things quickly. One day your baby won't be rolling over, but the next day he will. Even if your baby seems perfectly safe in his swing or bouncer seat, don't leave him unattended.

Also, never leave your baby unattended with a child under age five. Even an overzealous hug could cause injury.

Place bouncers on the ground. Never place your baby on an elevated surface, even if he's buckled into a bouncer seat or car-seat carrier. Even very young babies can lean forward or sideways, tip over a seat, and topple to the floor.

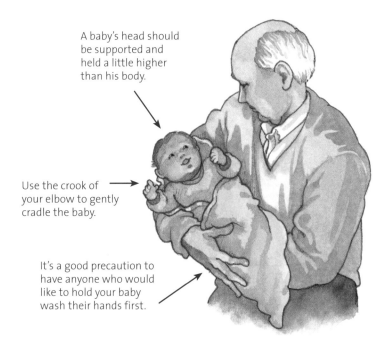

A baby's head should be supported and held a little higher than his body.

Use the crook of your elbow to gently cradle the baby.

It's a good precaution to have anyone who would like to hold your baby wash their hands first.

It is important that a baby is held safely at all times, so do not be shy about coaching the uninitiated a bit. Suggest the cradle hold for people unused to holding little ones. Cradling a baby is natural and simple. Place the baby's head in the crook of one of your arms and wrap your other arm around the baby.

Be size wise. Check the height and weight limits for your baby's products—such as his swing, bouncer seat, and bassinet—and make sure to stop using them once he exceeds them. Or stop using them once your baby starts trying to wriggle out of them.

Keep clean. Keep an eye out for what your baby puts into his mouth. He doesn't have the pincher grip yet, so he won't be picking up bits of lint, but he can grab larger objects. Watch out for small objects that he could choke on such as marbles, dangerous objects such as peeling paint, and germ-laden objects such as the dog's chew toy. Rinse anything that's been mouthed by another baby under hot running water.

Watch during tummy time. Because babies are put to sleep on their backs, their heads can develop flat spots, which is called plagiocephaly. To minimize this, pediatricians recommend plenty of tummy time—time on their bellies while they are awake. You'll want to watch your baby during tummy time for signs of sleepiness. If he looks sleepy, place him on his back in his crib.

Stay smoke free. Don't smoke or strike matches while holding a baby. Never leave burning cigarettes unattended.

Tummy time is important for back-sleeping babies, who have a tendency to develop flat spots on their heads.

Do not leave your baby unattended during her play time, particularly if she is lying on her tummy. A drowsy baby can fall asleep in a dangerous position, or she might be subjected to an unpleasant visit from the family pet.

Throughout the House

Once your baby is home, there are lots of things to do in other rooms of the house, and throughout the house, to keep her safe and sound.

Carry with care. As you carry your baby around the house, place one hand behind her head. It's terribly easy to bump her little head on doorframes, especially once she can whip it around to see what's going on.

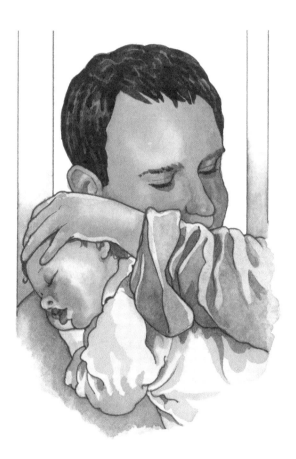

Always place a hand on your baby's head as you walk about the house. It is very easy to bump this fragile part of the body on objects as you pass by.

Be ready for emergencies. Remember that emergency room file you put together before your baby was born? Now that she's arrived, add the following to it:

- A description of her medical needs, including allergies, drug sensitivities, chronic conditions, and previous hospitalizations
- A list of any medications your baby takes
- Your baby's immunization records

Be on the lookout for choking hazards. Anything smaller than 1.68 inches (4.3 cm) in diameter—such as coins, deflated balloons and balloon parts, marbles, small toys, and nail scissors—is a choking hazard. If an object fits inside a toilet paper tube, it's small enough to pose a danger.

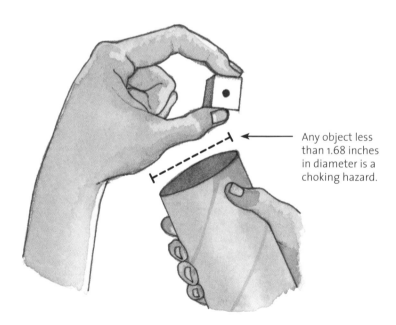

Any object less than 1.68 inches in diameter is a choking hazard.

A toilet paper tube is a handy babyproofing tool. If an object fits into the tube, it is a choking threat. Keep all such items safely away from your baby.

Safety Supplies: Small Parts Testers

These cylinder-shaped tubes allow you to test if an item is small enough for a baby to choke on—if the item fits inside the tube, it's too small. Also called "choke tubes," they cost around $2 at baby supplies stores.

Check toys carefully. Continue to look toys over carefully to make sure they're in good condition and remember to follow age recommendations. Especially as your baby learns how to put things into her mouth, check that toys have no buttons, eyes, beads, ribbons, or other pieces that your baby could pull off and choke on.

Cut tags off toys. Perhaps the chances are slim, but it's possible for a baby to cut her eye on the paper tags that list washing instructions on stuffed toys. Cut the tags off toys before giving them to your baby to play with.

Watch out for extension cords. "Don't place extension cords under rugs and carpet," says John Drengenberg, an electrical engineer and consumer affairs manager for Underwriters Laboratories, a nonprofit product safety certification organization. "People do this because they're trying to avoid a tripping hazard, but they're actually creating an even bigger hazard. Over time when people step on extension cords, they damage the wires. The carpet holds the heat in, and the carpet itself provides fuel for a fire to get started."

"Extension cords aren't a long-term solution," says Drengenberg. "They're meant for short-term use, such as for decorations during the holidays."

Don't wind or coil up electrical cords. "Although you might think you're doing a good thing—securing the cord so that it's not dangling over the edge of a counter-top where a child could grab it—repeatedly wrapping the cord can cause damage to the wires, which could ultimately start a fire," says Drengenberg.

Bag it. Discard plastic shopping and dry-cleaning bags right away. They are a suffocation hazard. Tie several knots in each bag before throwing it out.

Safety Alert: Hiring a Babysitter

Choosing the right babysitter is very important. Here are some tips:

- Find a safe sitter. If you hire a teenager to care for your baby, have her take a babysitting class. These are usually held at hospitals. The American Academy of Pediatrics has a good rule of thumb: The younger the child is, the older the sitter should be. Sitters should be at least thirteen years old.

- Preferably choose a sitter you know well and check references.

- Make sure the sitter will listen to your instructions. For example, she must place your baby to sleep on her back. If your babysitter is of an older generation, this may be surprising news. If you meet resistance, explain that it's your pediatrician's order or invite her on a visit to the pediatrician. Perhaps it will carry more weight coming from the doctor.

- Have the sitter brush up on baby-care skills by taking a baby care class. Information changes over time, and it's important to keep up with current knowledge. Even more important, she should take an infant CPR and first-aid class. These are all usually held at hospitals.

- Invite the sitter over before the first time you leave your baby with her. Show her the ropes, such where your list of emergency contact numbers is, how to change your baby's diaper, and what your baby's bedtime routine is.

- Write out detailed instructions for how you like things done, such as how to feed, diaper, and bathe your baby.

  "I watch my grandson, Tyler, once a week at my daughter's house while she works," says Mary Bright, a mother of two and professional crafter in Allentown, Pennsylvania. "She wrote lots of important information in a notebook, including her contact information, my grandson's pediatrician's number, and instructions on how to feed Tyler. It also includes less critical, but still helpful, information, such as how to play his DVDs."

- Practice your family's fire escape plan with the babysitter.

My Safety Story

Make sure that your child's caregivers know your safety rules. When my daughter was a baby, I had my entire house babyproofed. One of the first days I left her with her babysitter, however, I came home to discover that the babysitter needed to drive somewhere, and she took my daughter along, without a car seat! Her friend held my baby in the backseat. Thank goodness everything was fine.

—Karen Sheehan, M.D., M.P.H., medical director of the Injury Prevention and Research Center at Children's Memorial Hospital in Chicago

Safety Alert: Introducing Your Dog or Cat to Your Baby

Meeting your baby is an enormous event for your pet, especially if she was the spoiled only "child" before. Here's how to help ease her transition:

- Have your partner bring home something the baby wore, such as a hat or onesie, while you're both still in the hospital. This will help the pet familiarize herself with your baby's scent.
- The day you bring your baby home, have someone else carry the baby into another room while you warmly greet your pet for several minutes. When the pet is calm, have her sit next to you while you sit with the baby.
- Keep your baby and pet toys separate. Don't give your pet plush toys or rattles or she may mistake your baby's toys for her own.
- If your baby's crying makes your pet upset, encourage your pet to go to her safe retreat place.
- Watch your pet's response to your baby's crying. If she is distressed, consider letting your pet stay with a friend for the early weeks.
- Never leave your baby alone in a room with a pet.
- Close the door or gate to the nursery when your baby is in there unsupervised to keep the pet out.
- Reward your pet's good behavior with treats.

Outside

There's a great big world out there just waiting for your baby to discover. But you'll likely take baby steps, starting with your own backyard.

Keep cool. In hot weather, your baby is at risk for heat illness. Babies warm up fast and don't sweat efficiently. Plus they have more skin surface area relative to their weight to heat up in the sun than do older children. To beat the heat, dress your baby in loose-fitting, 100 percent cotton clothing. Babies are more susceptible than older children to dehydration, so breast- or bottle-feed him every hour.

Stay warm. Don't keep your baby outside for more than a few minutes when the temperature is below freezing. Dress him in several layers—one more than you are wearing. Change your baby's clothes right away if they get damp. Wet clothes can lead to frostnip.

Keep your baby out of the sun. Even on a cloudy or cold day, your baby's skin can be damaged by the sun. Up to 80 percent of children get sunburned each summer, and just one bad burn may double the risk of developing melanoma later in life.

A baby's skin is thinner than an adult's and more susceptible to sunburn. Before six months, a baby's own photoprotection is still underdeveloped, and sunburn can occur despite your best sun-protection efforts. It could take as little as ten to fifteen minutes for skin to burn. Protect your baby with a wide-brimmed hat, long sleeves, and pants. Keep him out of direct sunlight and in the shade as much as possible, especially between the peak hours of 10 a.m. and 3 p.m.

Take this test. To see whether your baby's clothes are sun-protective, hold them up to a lamp. The less light shining through, the better it'll be at blocking the sun's rays.

Safety Supplies: SuperBlankie

If your baby kicks off the blankets you place on him in the stroller or car seat, try a SuperBlankie. These soft blankets attach to the seat's harness with Velcro tabs, so they're easy to put on and come off with just one hand. You can buy them for around $10 at baby supplies websites.

KEEPING COOL

As much as possible, keep your baby in the shade.

A hat offers protection from the heat and the sun's damaging rays.

Opt for loose-fitting, light-colored, cotton clothing.

Keep your baby hydrated!

It's extremely important to guard against heat exhaustion. Babies do not have fully developed perspiration systems and can overheat and/or suffer from dehydration easily. The best plan of attack is to avoid the outdoors between 10 a.m. and 3 p.m. on the hottest summer days.

Be sun safe. If sun exposure is unavoidable, talk with your baby's pediatrician about using a touch of sunscreen on any exposed skin. Ask about using a product made specifically for babies. When you apply the sunscreen, be sure to keep it away from your baby's eyes and mouth. Until August 1999, the American Academy of Pediatrics warned against using sunscreen on babies younger than six months old. But now they say it's fine to use a small amount of sunscreen on a baby's face and hands. But cover up other skin with long sleeves, pants, and a hat.

Look for the seal of approval. To find the best sunscreen, look for the Skin Cancer Foundation's seal of approval. This means the product provides both UVA and UVB protection.

Choose sunscreen carefully. There are two types of sunscreen—chemical sunscreens that the skin absorbs and physical sunscreens, such as zinc oxide and titanium dioxide, that are supposed to sit on the top of the skin, forming a barrier against the sun's rays. However, because zinc oxide and titanium dioxide are normally opaque white, new versions of them in today's sunscreens use nano-sized particles. These particles are so small they're no longer visible, but lab studies indicate these nanoingredients create free radicals that damage the DNA of cells and could cause other harm as well. So you may want to consider avoiding sunscreens with zinc oxide or titanium dioxide altogether.

Plan ahead. Put sunscreen on your baby twenty to thirty minutes before going outside. It takes that long for the chemicals to work.

Reapply. Reapply sunscreen every two hours and after your baby has been sweating or in the water.

Shade those peepers. It's important to protect your baby's eyes from the sun. Try to avoid the sun at midday, when the UV rays are the strongest. When you can, make your own shade with a beach umbrella or stroller canopy.

You can buy snug-fitting wraparound sunglasses for babies. But if your baby won't stand for wearing sunglasses, a visor or hat that keeps the sun out of his eyes will help, too.

STROLLER SAFETY

Never use the stroller to hang parcels on; the stroller might tip over.

Always fasten *all* safety straps.

Beware of moving parts when folding and unfolding strollers. Your baby's fingers could get pinched.

Practice good stroller safety: Always buckle all straps, use the brakes when you stop, and don't leave your baby unattended. He might wriggle through the leg openings.

Stand clear. Keep your baby's fingers clear of your stroller when unfolding or folding it. Tiny fingers can get caught in the folding mechanisms. More than 11,000 children are injured by strollers each year, according to the U.S. Consumer Product Safety Commission.

Stay alert. When you're walking with your baby in his stroller, walk defensively. Motorists are supposed to yield to pedestrians in crosswalks, but they often don't. Keep your stroller far back from the road while waiting to cross and always look left, right, left before stepping into the street. If you must walk on a roadway because sidewalks are unavailable, walk facing the oncoming traffic so you can take evasive action if a vehicle comes into your path. Be especially careful in parking lots and garages.

Buckle up. Even if you're just walking a few steps, always fasten your baby into his stroller. It doesn't take much of a bump in the road for a baby to bounce out.

Don't handle it. Don't hang a purse or shopping bag over the stroller handle. The weight could cause the stroller to tip over.

Watch your baby in the stroller. Don't leave your baby unattended in the stroller, especially if he's sleeping. Babies can wriggle down through the leg openings.

Don't let go. If you stop with your stroller, apply the brakes. But keep one hand on the stroller just in case, especially if you're parked on a hill.

Strike a pose. Always have a recent photo of your baby with you. It can be a useful source of identification in case your child is lost. Update the photo every four months for your baby's first two years because babies grow and change so quickly.

Choosing the Safest Day Care

One major place your baby might go outside of your home is day care. Choosing your child's day care provider is a huge decision, and safety is a major factor. Here are some things to consider:

- What is the child-staff ratio? To see if the center meets state guidelines, check with your state's Department of Children and Family Services or Department of Social Services.

- Do all staff members have training in first aid and infant CPR?

- Have all staff members had a recent exam and immunizations?

- Do all members of the staff speak English well enough to handle an emergency?

- Does the center have working smoke alarms and carbon monoxide alarms?

- Does the center have a plan for evacuation in case of an emergency?

- Does the center look clean?

- Is the center well-ventilated?

- Is the sound level comfortable?
- Are babies in swings, strollers, and high chairs strapped in?
- Does the gear look to be safe and in good working order?
- Do caregivers place infants to sleep on their backs? (A disproportionate one-fifth of Sudden Infant Death Syndrome cases occur in child care settings. And shockingly, more than 20 percent of babies in day care centers are still put to sleep on their bellies.)
- Are the cribs free of blankets, toys, and other hazards?
- Does each child have his or her own bedding for naps?
- Are sleeping children within view of caregivers, are doors to napping areas left open, or are monitors used?
- Are there safety straps on the changing tables?
- Is the diaper changing area clean and does it have disposable gloves and a sink nearby?

PART III

Six Months to One Year

UH OH, HERE WE GO, YOUR BABY IS SITTING BY HERSELF, CRAWLING, AND STANDING NOW. SHE CAN REACH THINGS ON LOW TABLES, CRAWL ACROSS THE ROOM TOWARD THE LAMP'S CORD, AND TRY TO PULL HERSELF UP USING THE DOG'S FUR.

"BY THE TIME YOUR BABY TURNS SIX MONTHS OLD, CRAWL AROUND YOUR HOUSE TO GET A VIEW FROM YOUR SOON-TO-BE TODDLER'S PERSPECTIVE," SAYS MARJORIE HOGAN, M.D., DIRECTOR OF PEDIATRIC MEDICAL EDUCATION AT THE HENNEPIN COUNTY MEDICAL CENTER IN MINNEAPOLIS AND ASSOCIATE PROFESSOR OF PEDIATRICS AT THE UNIVERSITY OF MINNESOTA. "THAT'S HOW TO BEST IDENTIFY WHAT SHARP CORNERS NEED TO BE PADDED, WHICH CABINETS NEED TO BE LATCHED, AND WHAT NEEDS TO BE MOVED OUT OF HER REACH."

IN GENERAL AT THIS AGE, DISTRACTION WORKS WELL. DIVERT YOUR BABY'S ATTENTION FROM SOMETHING FORBIDDEN WITH SOMETHING SHE CAN PLAY WITH. TRY USING A NEGATIVE VOICE AND EYE CONTACT. GIVE ATTENTION WHEN YOUR BABY IS BEHAVING WELL, RATHER THAN WHEN SHE IS CRYING OR MISBEHAVING.

AT THIS TIME YOUR BABY MIGHT APPEAR TO BE IGNORING YOU. MORE LIKELY, SHE'S JUST DISTRACTED BY WHATEVER IT IS SHE'S DOING. TRY TO EXPLAIN WHAT YOU'RE DOING TO YOUR BABY, EVEN IF SHE'S TOO YOUNG TO UNDERSTAND. FOR EXAMPLE, IF YOU'RE MOVING HER AWAY FROM THE DOG'S FOOD BOWL TOWARD HER PILE OF BLOCKS, EXPLAIN THAT THE BLOCKS ARE HER TOYS TO PLAY WITH.

"REMEMBER THAT IT'S NORMAL FOR A BABY TO EXPLORE, TO TRY NEW THINGS, AND ALSO FOR HER TO WATCH WHAT YOUR REACTION WILL BE WHEN SHE DOES NEW THINGS," SAYS DR. HOGAN. "GIVE HER PLENTY OF OPPORTUNITIES TO DO THAT. CHILDREN ARE LIKE LITTLE SCIENTISTS."

The Nursery

Your baby still spends a lot of time in her nursery, napping during the day and sleeping at night. It's critical to make it a safe place for her.

Remove bumper pads. Once your baby tries to pull herself to a standing position, remove the bumper pads so she can't use them to climb out of her crib. Take out any large toys that could be used as steps as well.

Although consider these bumper pads. If your baby likes to stick her hand and feet out of the crib and you worry about them getting stuck, you can buy mesh bumpers that keep the baby's head and limbs inside the crib. They cost around $25 through baby safety supplies catalogs.

Lower the crib mattress. As soon as your baby is able to stand, lower the crib mattress.

Now that your baby can stand, it is time to lower the mattress to a safer height.

Bumper pads and crib toys are no longer a good idea—your baby could try to use these to climb out!

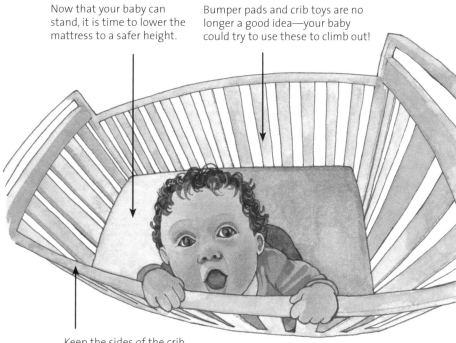

Keep the sides of the crib raised and locked in place.

A seven- to-twelve-month-old baby is beginning to pull up, stand, and even climb. It is time to recheck the nursery for objects that she might reach or that might serve as a boost to escape from her crib.

Lock the sides. Especially now that she's trying to pull herself up, when your baby is in her crib, make sure the drop side of the crib is up and locked.

Check the crib placement. Make sure window blinds and drapery are far out of the baby's reach, preferably on another wall.

Undeck the walls. If you have any wall decorations with ribbons or streamers, remove them or move them away from your baby's crib and places where she plays to prevent entanglement.

Hang on tighter. Between seven and twelve months, diaper changes become more challenging as your baby practices rolling over. When your baby learns how to crawl, diaper changes really become an adventure. She'll want to crawl away. Be sure to keep a hand on your baby while changing her diaper and always use the changing table's safety strap. And of course, never leave her unattended on her changing table.

Be a master of distraction. To help keep your baby safely on the changing table, keep her distracted. Keep a favorite toy on the changing table or hang a detailed and colorful poster by the changing table. Tell her stories, chew gum and blow bubbles, or sing her songs, anything to keep her occupied long enough for you to—quickly—change her diaper.

Create a safety zone. Move heavy and dangerous objects at least 12 inches (30 cm) away from your baby's changing table so they're safely out of reach from her curious hands.

Paint with care. If you repaint a child's toy or furniture, use only paint labeled "non-toxic."

Bolt it down. Once your baby is starting to pull herself up on, and soon crawl up on, furniture, secure it to the floor and/or walls.

"When my son, Evan, started to pull himself up on things, I moved his changing table out of his room," says Marie Suszynski, a mother of one and freelance writer in Emmaus, Pennsylvania. "He can climb up it in about two seconds. I'm going to attach his dresser to the wall for the day that he learns to open the drawers and use those as steps for climbing. We started using time-outs when he tries to climb something that he shouldn't. I put him in his exersaucer for a minute and tell him, 'You need a time out because you're not listening to me when I tell you that you can't climb onto the table.' It seems to be working."

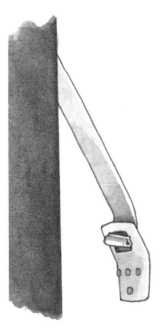

Taller, heavy furniture poses a hazard to the older baby who uses it to try to pull herself up to an upright position. It is more important than ever to anchor shelves and dressers to the wall for extra security. Hardware stores and babyproofing suppliers have many products available for this purpose.

Check toys carefully. Continue to look toys over carefully to make sure they're in good condition, free of pieces that your baby could pull off and choke on, and age appropriate. As your baby learns to stand, make sure that toys aren't too heavy. If a toy would harm your baby if it fell onto her, it's too heavy.

Don't give your baby—or any child under age eight—toys that need to plug into an electrical outlet. Use battery-operated toys instead.

Play safely. Each time your baby gets a new toy, show her how to play with it safely.

Toss the wrappings. As soon as you open a toy, discard the plastic wrappings. They could suffocate a child. Throw out the plastic straps and bolts, too, because they can be choking hazards.

Play keep away. If you have older children, teach them to keep their toys away from younger siblings. Help them to understand that their toys may contain small parts that younger children could swallow. Be especially on the alert for toys with small parts, magnets, or stickers.

Lower the noise. Toy noise can damage your baby's hearing. A toy shouldn't be louder than a blender, about 90 decibels. It should be even softer if it's meant to be held close to the ear, such as a toy phone. Yet it's not uncommon for noisy squeak toys to be 135 decibels, louder than an ambulance siren. You can buy a sound-level meter to check your baby's toys at an electronics store for around $40. The simplest way to reduce the noise? Take out the batteries.

Inspect toys. Regularly check your baby's toys for signs of wear or damage. A good time to do this might be when you put her toys away for the day. Look for sharp or jagged edges, weak seams, and broken parts that could pose a choking hazard. Sand any sharp or splintered surfaces on wooden toys. Repair any toys that you can and discard those that you can't.

Avoid vending machine toys. They might contain lead. Also vending machine toys don't have to meet safety regulations, and they often contain small parts. Similarly, toys sold or given away at carnivals and fairs may not be labeled as choking hazards.

Stay dry. Never use open buckets filled with water as diaper pails. Your baby could stand up next to it, fall in, and drown.

Check out toy chests. "If you have any type of boxes in the baby's room, such as a toy chest or window seat with storage, be sure the lid has a safety hinge and breathing holes," says Shalena Smith, owner of Ga Ga Designs, a Los Angeles–based interior design company that specializes in nurseries and kids' rooms. "This is critical for anything a child might try to hide in."

And make sure the chest is nonlocking. Better yet, buy a chest with a detached lid or doors. Make sure the chest's ventilation holes won't be blocked if the chest is placed against a wall in case a child climbs into the chest.

THE TOY CHEST

Chests with lids should be equipped with safety hinges. (Better yet, choose a container without a lid.)

Ventilation holes are important, in case your child gets trapped inside.

Store your baby's stuffed animals and toys safely outside the crib to avoid potential problems such as strangulation and suffocation. While a toy chest might seem like a good solution, it too can present safety hazards if not chosen wisely.

The Kitchen

"Of all of the rooms in the house, the kitchen poses extra risks to kids," says Garry Gardner, M.D., a pediatrician in private practice in Darien, Illinois, and former member of the American Academy of Pediatrics Committee on Injury, Violence, and Poison Prevention. "There are lots of babyproofing gadgets you can use, but the bottom line is you must supervise your baby in the kitchen. Don't trust a baby to be careful and never leave a baby alone in the kitchen. One of the biggest problems in the kitchen is that parents tend to be busy and distracted there. And it takes only seconds for an injury to occur. That moment you turn away, an awful thing can happen."

Prevent burns and scalds. Safe Kids USA estimates that most scald burns, especially among kids from six months to two years, are from hot foods and liquids spilled in the kitchen. So, for example, don't let your baby near the coffeepot, hot water heater, fry food cooker, or their cords.

Move dangerous substances. "Rather than keeping dangerous products such as cleansers in a low cabinet with a child lock, keep them up high with the child lock," says Nancy A. Cowles, director of Kids in Danger, a nonprofit organization dedicated to protecting children by improving children's product safety. "Children have been known to outsmart childproof locks. Appropriate supervision is the best protection."

Plus it's important to lock even high cabinets because later on it's not impossible for a child to move a chair over to a counter to gain access to high cabinets.

Even after you move the products from under the sink, lock up the cabinet. After years of chemicals being stored there, the cabinet floor can be saturated with them. If your baby reaches in there with a wet hand, the poisons can be reactivated.

Distract. Lock all of the lower-level cabinets, except for one. Choose the cabinet farthest from the stove. Stock that one with lightweight, safe items, such as plastic refrigerator dishes. That will help to distract your crawler from forbidden places.

"Make sure there are things at your toddler's level that she can play with, such as a cabinet filled with only Tupperware containers in the kitchen," says Marjorie Hogan, M.D., director of pediatric medical education at the Hennepin County Medical Center in Minneapolis and associate professor of pediatrics at the University of Minnesota. "Create a space like this in each room."

Store things in their original containers. Don't transfer products such as cleaning supplies into unlabeled bottles. You might not remember what's in them and certainly your baby won't. Most important, never put nonfood items into containers that were once used for food.

Salt with care. Keep salt out of your baby's reach. Just a tablespoon and a half of ordinary table salt can kill a small child.

Lock up look-alikes. Many household products look a lot like tempting treats to kids. In the kitchen, for example, Windex looks a lot like Gatorade. Be especially careful to lock these look-alikes up.

Safety Supplies: Cabinet Latches

There's a wide array of cabinet latches out there. You'll find regular screw-mounted latches, but also self-adhesive latches, latches that mount on the outside of cabinets for corner cabinets and lazy-Susan-style doors, and magnetic locks.

"You can buy simple lock systems for cabinets and drawers that can be installed according to the directions on the package with just a screwdriver, and sometimes even no tools at all," says Angel Pendleton, a mother of four and a franchisee of the House Doctors Handyman Service.

"When putting latches on kitchen cabinets and drawers, don't forget to put a latch on the drawer holding Ziploc bags, aluminum foil, and Saran Wrap," says Holly Silvestri, a mother of twins in Las Vegas, Nevada. "Many of the edges on these boxed items have cutters on them. They could be dangerous if a child gets a hold of them."

Move sharp objects and other hazards, too. Other important things to move include knives, matches, plastic bags, and refrigerator magnets.

Create a safety zone. Move heavy and dangerous objects at least 12 inches (30 cm) away from table and counter edges so they're safely out of reach from your baby's curious hands.

Corral cords. Don't let appliance cords dangle off of countertops. Keep appliance cords retracted into the appliances or tucked behind them so your baby can't pull down toasters, coffeemakers, and other appliances.

Beware of deep fryers. "After a person cooks with a deep fryer, it's easy to let it sit on the counter to cool," says John Drengenberg, an electrical engineer and consumer affairs manager for Underwriters Laboratories (UL), a nonprofit product safety certification organization. "A child could grab the cord, pulling the hot oil down on himself, causing terrible burns. Be sure to move the deep fryer and cord far from the edge of the counter and supervise your child near it."

"Consider replacing older deep fryers," says Drengenberg. "UL has developed standards for a new type of cord that pulls free from the fryer when the cord is pulled on, to prevent the fryer and oil from falling."

CABINET SAFETY

Cabinet latches keep
your curious baby out
and precious objects in.

Give your baby a chance
to explore in at least one
of your cabinets. Make
sure the objects in it are
unbreakable and safe.

Cabinet latches serve to keep your breakables safe from your baby's curious hands, but more important they keep him away from possible dangers such as toxic cleaners, breakable pottery and glass, and knives and other sharp objects.

Unplug. When you're not using appliances—such as coffeemakers, toasters, and mixers—keep them unplugged. Even when an appliance is turned off, if it's plugged in, it can have dangerous electrical voltages inside of it.

Use the least-toxic products possible. Consider using nonchlorine bleaches, vinegar, borax, beeswax, mineral oil, and compressed-air drain openers (instead of corrosive liquids). Products with labels that say "caution" or "warning" are less toxic than ones that read "danger" or "poison."

Watch cleaning products. When you're cleaning or using household chemicals, don't leave the bottles unattended. If possible, clean while your baby is napping or away from home. Statistic show that unintentional exposure to toxic cleaning supplies usually happens between 4 p.m. and 8 p.m.

Lock up the dishwasher. Place a lock on the dishwasher so your baby can't reach inside and grab the steak knives and other sharp objects. Or at least keep the dishwasher closed and latched when it's not in being loaded and unloaded.

Load the dishwasher right. Point knives and forks down in the utensil basket of the dishwasher so your child can't grab the sharp edges.

Wait to add soap. Fill the dishwasher with soap right before you run it and wipe out any leftover detergent after the load is done. Dishwasher detergent is extremely corrosive and dangerous. It can irritate a child's skin and eyes and burn the lining of his mouth and esophagus if swallowed.

Store soap carefully. Place the cap back on the dishwasher detergent tightly and store it in a locked—preferably high—cabinet.

Keep your baby away from the dishwasher. The dishwasher itself has pointy spikes on the rack that can harm your baby if he falls on them. Keep him away when you're loading and unloading dishes.

DISHWASHER SAFETY

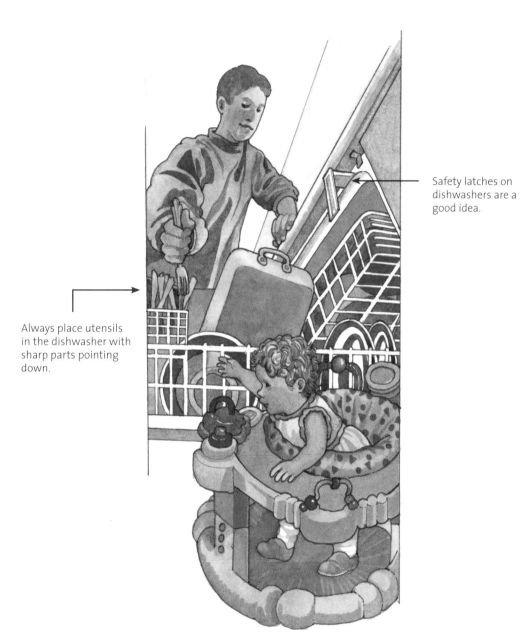

Safety latches on dishwashers are a good idea.

Always place utensils in the dishwasher with sharp parts pointing down.

An open dishwasher can pose many hazards, from sharp objects to corrosive cleaners. Never let your baby explore around an open dishwasher door.

Safety Supplies: Refrigerator Locks

To keep curious kids out of the fridge, consider buying a fridge lock. They mount to the top of the refrigerator and open with the press of a button. They cost around $6 in baby safety supplies catalogs.

Keep away. Do not allow your baby near the stove, says Dr. Gardner. Even after the heat is turned off, the oven and stove can still be hot.

Create a safety zone of at least 3 feet (1 m) around the stove during, and right after, cooking. If you replace your stove, consider getting a new, better-insulated one, which should stay cooler.

Tip-proof your stove. Toddlers have been critically injured by tipping over stoves and doused with pots of scalding water. Consider securing the stove to the wall with a wall anchor or safety strap. Make sure your range is properly installed with anti-tip brackets. These secure the rear legs to the floor. Manufacturers are required to provide these brackets on ranges made after 1991. If yours is older than that, contact the company for the parts or order them from an appliance-parts store. To test yours, grab the back of the oven and pull forward and open the oven door and push down. The oven shouldn't tip forward.

Keep the oven door closed. Whenever you're not using the oven, keep the door closed. And certainly never let your baby climb on an open oven door.

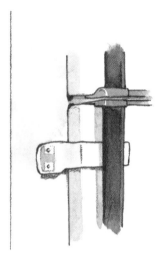

Clever refrigerator locks will keep the active baby from climbing shelves and the curious one from tasting food items.

Don't touch. Don't let your baby touch hot water spigots, even when they are cool. He might touch them once safely but get burned the next time.

Dish it out. Don't serve your baby food on imported or glazed pottery or ceramic dishes or store your food in it. They can leach lead into food.

Beware of tablecloths. Overhanging tablecloths and large placemats are easily grabbed and pulled down by babies. This is especially dangerous if breakable dishes, hot food, or sharp knives are still on them.

Keep keys away. Don't allow your baby to chew on keys. Besides the obvious germ factor, old brass keys can contain small amounts of lead.

Safety Supplies: Stove Guards, Knobs, and Locks

A stove guard, which costs around $23 and is available from safety supply catalogs, keeps kids from touching hot burners.

"My son, Evan, loves to reach for things on the kitchen counter, and once he started standing and walking I was amazed at what he could reach," says Marie Suszynski, a mother of one and freelance writer in Emmaus, Pennsylvania. I've been nervous about the stove since he was born, so I bought a plastic guard to put at the front edge of the stove to keep Evan from being able to put his hand up on a burner. As a bonus, it catches splatters from hot food."

If your stove knobs are on the front of your stove, they're easily accessible to kids. You can buy hinged, plastic covers that lock over the knobs. You can hear them "click" into place. They cost around $9 for a set of five from baby safety supplies catalogs.

You can buy heat-resistant locks specially designed for oven doors, which cost around $4 from baby safety supplies catalogs. They adhere with special tape. Adults can open them with squeeze-and-release tabs.

STOVE SAFETY

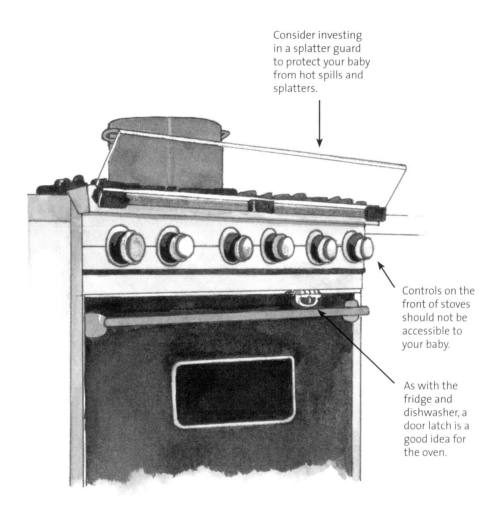

Consider investing in a splatter guard to protect your baby from hot spills and splatters.

Controls on the front of stoves should not be accessible to your baby.

As with the fridge and dishwasher, a door latch is a good idea for the oven.

Equip your stove with the latest safety products and exercise extreme caution whenever your baby is nearby and you're cooking.

Keep purses out of reach. Move purses, and also luggage, to high shelves or in a secured closet. Put guests' bags in a safe place as well. They are likely to contain things dangerous to babies, such as lipstick and medicine.

Move recyclables. Place bins for glass and metal containers behind a locked door, or better yet outside.

"Watch out for sharp objects," says Dr. Gardner. "For example, if you open up a can and put the can and dangling lid into the trash can, your baby could reach into the garbage can and cut himself on the sharp edges."

Be clean. Especially in the kitchen, be careful about small things that fall on the floor. A baby is quick to snatch up seemingly harmless things like dry beans or peas and push them into his nose or ear, where they can swell up and cause untold misery, or into his mouth, where they can be choking hazards.

Twist off. Drink a lot of bottled water? Consider switching to a brand such as Deer Park, which sells water in bottles with twist open, not twist off, caps. Those little white caps are a choking hazard.

Place the high chair right. Don't put your baby's high chair in a place where his waving arms or grabbing hands can reach anything.

Take a step. Get a skidproof step stool. With close supervision, your curious baby can sit on it—and later stand—to watch you prepare meals.

Wash up. Fingers pick up germs from surfaces and other people, and whenever you touch your eyes, mouth, or nose, the germs get into your body. Teach your baby to wash his hands the right way to prevent the spread of germs. Typically, people don't wash their hands long enough. You have to rub vigorously with soap and water to break the germs away from your skin.

For now, your baby will need assistance doing this. Help him wet his hands and apply soap. Then help him rub his hands together, scrubbing for twenty seconds, or the length of "Happy Birthday" sung twice. Help him rinse his hands, and then dry them well with a clean towel.

FEEDING TIME

Clean the jar before opening. Do not serve food from the jar. Instead, transfer contents as needed to a clean bowl and refrigerate any *untouched* leftovers in the jar immediately.

Choose a spoon with a plastic tip and no sharp edges.

Keep the high chair clean and germ-free.

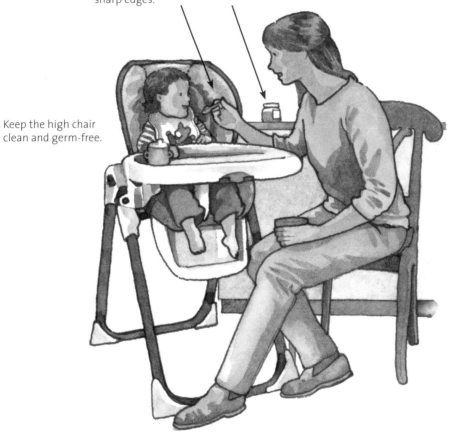

A few precautions will ensure that your baby's feeding time is a pleasure. Take your time and feed soft foods to avoid choking. Always allow hot food to cool to a safe temperature.

Safety Alert: Feeding

By four to six months, most babies can digest solid food, which is when your baby's pediatrician will likely suggest adding it. Signs that your baby is ready include his interest in your food and good head, neck, and upper-body control. Starting to eat solid food is a big deal to your baby, and it's a big safety issue as well. Choking is a leading cause of accidental death among infants.

- Store unopened baby food in a clean, cool, dry place.
- Choose a quiet time to feed your baby when you can give him your full attention.
- Before feeding your baby, wash your hands and his hands.
- Wipe the tops of baby food jars or run them under water to remove dust before opening.
- Make sure the button is down on safety lids before opening a jar for the first time and listen for the pop to indicate the seal was intact.
- Store your baby's feeding supplies—such as bibs, food, spoons, and wipes—nearby so you don't have to leave him alone to fetch them.
- Strap your baby into his high chair. He'll be able to swallow better if he's sitting down.
- Note where your baby's fingers are before attaching the tray so you don't pinch them.
- Pull your baby's high chair so that he's facing you so you can watch him eat. Be sure to snap the tray in place because it will prevent him from launching forward and bonking his head on the table.

- Consider buying organic baby food. According to a study from the Organic Center for Education and Promotion in Greenfield, Massachusetts, certain fruits and vegetables contain higher levels of pesticide residues than others. These include apples, nectarines, peaches, pears, strawberries, celery, spinach, squash, and sweet bell peppers. Consider buying the organic versions of these foods.

- Transfer jarred foods into a separate container before serving them to your baby, using a clean spoon or fork. Once food comes into contact with saliva, it's contaminated with bacteria, so you must discard it. Even if the food is refrigerated, this bacteria can grow in the food or drink and make your baby sick if he eats it later.

- Choose foods appropriate for your baby's development. At this age, all foods should be strained or mushy. Your baby isn't so much chewing now; he presses the food against the top of his mouth and then swallows.

- Use a rubber-tipped spoon to avoid injuring your baby's gums.

- Check that your baby's food isn't too hot. Stir and cool food before serving. It's best not to heat food in the microwave because it can cause hot spots.

- Place just a small amount of food on the tip of the spoon.

- Feed your baby slowly and watch him carefully for choking and gagging.

- Clean the high chair well after feeding your baby with soapy water.

Safety Alert: Feeding (continued)

By the time your baby is around nine month old, he can eat some table food such as crackers and round toasted oat cereal, crunchy foods that dissolve quickly such as baby biscuits or crackers, small pieces of cooked pasta, cooked vegetables (such as halved peas and finely chopped potatoes and carrots), and mashed fruits (such as applesauce and bananas).

Even if your baby has only a few teeth, he can chew. Gums are mighty strong on their own, which you're likely well aware of if your baby has ever tried to use your finger for a teething ring.

- Protect your baby from food poisoning. Carefully check expiration dates, keep your kitchen clean and bug free, wash produce well, fully cook meat and poultry, and keep prepared foods away from raw meat, chicken, and eggs.

- Give your baby foods that are appropriate for his development. When in doubt, your pediatrician should be a great source of information on this.

- Cut food up into very small pieces. One danger at this age is that a baby's front teeth can bite off a chunk of food, but he can't actually chew it up.

- Avoid foods that could lodge in a child's throat. Many of them are things that people commonly think of as children's foods. The following foods are unsafe for kids under age three:

  - Apples (raw)
  - Berries, cherries, and grapes (whole)
  - Cheese cubes
  - Candy (chewy ones, such as caramels, and hard ones, such as mints)
  - Corn nuts
  - Fruit (dried)
  - Gum
  - Hot dogs or other meat chunks
  - Jelly beans
  - Marshmallows
  - Nuts (such as peanuts, almonds, and cashews)
  - Peanut butter
  - Pears (raw)
  - Peas (whole)
  - Popcorn
  - Raisins
  - Seeds
  - Watermelon with seeds
  - Vegetables (raw, such as carrots and celery)

- Consider these safer finger foods:
  - Avocado (small cubes of peeled, ripe)
  - Couscous (plain variety)
  - Hummus
  - Mango (very ripe, small pieces)
  - Orzo (well-cooked tiny pasta)
  - Tofu (small cubes of semi-firm)
- You should avoid giving these other foods to your baby, not be-cause of choking, but for other safety reasons:
  - Cow's milk: Your baby can't digest the protein in cow's milk, it doesn't contain all the nutrients he needs, and it contains high amounts of minerals that can damage his kidneys.
  - Eggs: Egg whites may cause an allergic reaction. Wait until your baby's first birthday before giving him egg whites. Cooked egg yolks are fine. (You might want to talk with your baby's pediatrician about this one if you'd like your baby to have some birthday cake on his first birthday! He or she might suggest trying eggs out a few weeks before your baby's birthday.)
  - Homemade baby food made of beets, carrots, collard greens, spinach, or turnips: Store-bought versions of these vegetables are safe, but these vegetables contain nitrates that in large amounts can harm a baby under age one.
  - Honey: It may contain botulism spores, which can be toxic to a baby. (Honey is fine when it's baked into foods.)
  - Nuts: If you or your baby's other parent is allergic to peanuts or tree nuts such as pecans and walnuts, wait until your baby is at least three before giving him peanuts or tree nuts. The earlier these foods are introduced to your baby, the better the chances are they'll become lifelong allergens for some kids.
  - Salt: Large quantities of salt can result in salt poisoning or seizures.
  - Shellfish: If you or your baby's other parent is allergic to shell-fish, wait until he is three or four before giving it to him.
  - Strawberries: Raw strawberries cause some kids to break out in rashes. If you're concerned, give your baby cooked berries until he's a year old.

Safety Alert: Feeding (continued)

- Wheat: If you're worried about allergies, wait to give your baby wheat until after his first birthday.
- Unpasteurized cheese or juice: Pasteurization removes harmful bacteria.
- Never leave your baby alone while he's eating or drinking. While it's tempting to use this time to catch up on chores, it's important that you be there watching in case he chokes or gags.
- Don't continue feeding your baby if he is resisting or crying, because that makes it easier for him to choke.
- Brush up on what to do if your baby chokes. Ask your baby's pediatrician to demonstrate what to do or take a first-aid class. You can order a pamphlet on first aid, choking, and CPR from the American Academy of Pediatrics website (www.aap.org).
- Discard any food uneaten from the dish.

Around eleven months, your baby will probably start to learn how to use utensils. It's your job to make sure he does it safely.

- Choose a spoon that's soft on his gums, sized for his mouth, and curved to help him get his food to his mouth.

- Consider buying a training plate with suction cups to keep it stable and curved sides that make it easy to scoop up food. And of course, it should be break-resistant plastic, never glass.

- Offer your toddler easy-to-spoon cut-up or mashed food.

Buckle up. Around ten months, your baby may develop a rebellious streak, and resist being strapped into his high chair. No matter how tempting it might be to give in, don't. It's important to buckle him in each and every time. Don't rely on the tray as a restraining device. Babies can slip down under the trays.

Stay close. Never leave your baby unattended in his high chair.

Stop! Don't let your child eat while crawling or standing.

Safety Supplies: Heat-Indicator Utensils

Consider special forks and spoons that tell you if the food is too hot by with tips that turn white. You can buy them for around $3 at baby supplies stores

The Bathroom

Once your baby is crawling around and wanting to explore everything, the easiest thing to do is keep the bathroom door closed, at least until she can stand and operate the door knob. Most important—never leave your baby alone in a bathroom.

Move medications. Medicines needs to be out of reach, says Charles Shubin, M.D., director of pediatrics at Mercy FamilyCare in Baltimore, Maryland. Childproof containers are really almost adultproof and only a deterrent to the determined child.

Place prescription and nonprescription medications and vitamins in upper-level cabinets and lock them. It's important to lock the cabinets because later on it's not impossible for a child to climb up on the bathroom vanity to gain access to high cabinets.

Move other toxic items as well. Even seemingly benign products such as mouthwash and iron pills can be dangerous to a young child. According to the National Capital Poison Center, the majority of calls to poison centers for young children involve hair-care, cosmetic, and other personal care items. Be careful where you store medicines, and especially vitamins containing iron, as they account for 30 percent of pediatric poisoning deaths. In addition, many mouthwashes contain substantial amounts of alcohol.

Everyday items such as nail polish, lipstick, powder, and other cosmetics and topical creams and lotions are dangerous as well. Look out for products such as perm and hair-straightening products, which can burn skin.

"Poisonings are a danger in bathrooms," says Garry Gardner, M.D., a pediatrician in private practice in Darien, Illinois, and former member of the American Academy of Pediatrics Committee on Injury, Violence, and Poison Prevention. "Keep only products that you use every day—such as mouthwash and tooth-paste—in the bathroom, out of your toddler's reach. Move everything else—such as medications, hair-coloring supplies, and cleaning products—to another room, out of your toddler's reach, and locked up. These items should be out of your toddler's sight and out of her mind."

Look out for look-alikes. Many household products look a lot like tempting treats to kids. For example, Sudafed looks like red-hot cinnamon candy. Be especially careful to lock these look-alikes up.

Store things in their original containers. Don't transfer products such as nail polish remover into unlabeled bottles. You might not remember what's in them and certainly your child won't. Most important, never put nonfood items into containers that were once used for food.

Request child-resistant packaging. Ask the pharmacist for these safer packages for all medications. Still, keep all medicine out of your baby's reach. Child-resistant doesn't equal childproof.

Toss the ipecac. In the past, experts recommended keeping syrup of ipecac on hand to induce vomiting if someone swallowed something poisonous. Not anymore. These days it's rarely recommended, and the National Capital Poison center says it is not necessary to keep ipecac syrup in your home.

That's because there's no evidence that vomiting actually removes poison from a child's body. Emergency rooms have stopped using ipecac and now administer activated charcoal, which binds to poisons in the stomach and prevents them from entering the bloodstream. Another problem with ipecac is that if you give your baby ipecac and she's continually vomiting, she may be unable to tolerate activated charcoal or other poison treatments at the hospital.

In case of poisoning, call the American Association of Poison Control Centers at 800-222-1222.

Don't treat medicine or vitamins like candy. Don't refer to medicine as candy and don't take your own medicine when your baby is around to see. Be cautious using vitamins that look like candy.

Pitch it. Dispose of unused, old, or expired medicines. But don't flush them down the toilet or pour them down the sink where they can contaminate the water supply. If you live in the United States, ask your city or county waste disposal agency whether there's a program in place to safely get rid of them. Or ask your pharmacist whether he will take expired drugs.

If all else fails, leave the medicine in its original container, seal it in a plastic bag, and stow it safely out of reach until trash collection day. Then take it directly outside to your garbage can.

Keep bath and baby oils out of your baby's reach. Bath and baby oils, massage oils, and other household and cosmetics products containing liquid hydrocarbons can cause a condition like pneumonia, irreversible lung damage, and even death if a child aspirates it into her lungs.

Keep mineral oil out of your baby's reach. Similar to liquid hydrocarbons, mineral oil can be dangerous. Keep mineral oil, and products containing it such as cold cream, out of your baby's reach. Even some baby products, such as Aquaphor ointment, contain mineral oil.

Create a safety zone. Move heavy and dangerous objects—such as hair dryers, curling irons, and razors—at least 12 inches (30 cm) away from bathroom counter edges so they're safely out of reach from your baby's curious hands.

Unplug. When you're not using appliances, such as curling irons and hair dryers, keep them unplugged. Even when an appliance is turned off, if it's plugged in, it can have dangerous electrical voltages inside of it.

Don't let your baby touch hot water spigots. She might touch them once safely when they are cool, but get burned the next time when they are hot.

Safety Supplies: Bathtub Spout and Knob Covers and Drain Covers

Padded cushion covers for the faucet and hot and cold knobs cost around $13 through baby safety supplies catalogs. They shield your baby from scratches, bumps, and bruises in the tub.

You can also buy a drain valve cover to keep your baby from pinching her fingers in the tub drain. They cost around $7 in baby safety supplies catalogs.

Safety Supplies: Toilet Locks

Unlike most adults, whose weight is concentrated around their bellies, a baby's weight is concentrated in the top half of her body. If a baby leans over to peer into a toilet bowl, she can lose her balance, fall forward, and drown. Or if a baby can open the lid, the lid may fall down on her fingers, or (ick) she may play in the toilet water.

Toilet locks are plastic devices that keep the lids down, but they open easily for adults and older kids. They cost around $10 at major retailers.

Put the lid down. At this age, few toys are more fascinating to a baby than the toilet. It can be swished in, and it is an excellent receptacle to drop toys into.

To prevent your baby's access to water, keep toilet lids down. Consider using a toilet lock to keep your baby from opening the lid. (See above for more on locks.)

Clean right. Don't use colored automatic toilet bowl cleaners in your toilet. The blue color will make the toilet water even more attractive to your baby, and the chemicals they contain are very dangerous.

Don't let children in spas, hot tubs, or Jacuzzis. Their bodies are more sensitive to hot water.

Don't use a bath seat. These devices have been associated with approximately 120 drownings and 160 injuries since 1983. The suction cups that hold the seat secure to the tub can come unstuck, and the seat can tip over, which can make the baby hit her head on the tub or go under water. This is especially common in tubs with slip-proof surfaces. Or babies can slip out of the seats into the water and become submerged. Unfortunately, these devices can give parents a false sense of security. Bath seats are bathing aids, not safety devices. Most manufacturers have stopped making them.

"I was running a tub of bath water and had put my baby in the seat that suctioned to the bottom of the tub. I just stepped to the next room for a bottle of shampoo and in that 3 seconds, he had tipped over and was face-first in the flow of water," says Angel Pendleton, a mother of four and a franchisee of the House Doctors Handyman Service. "Thankfully he was fine."

Toilet Safety

Locks for the toilets in your home can be a wise investment when little ones are around.

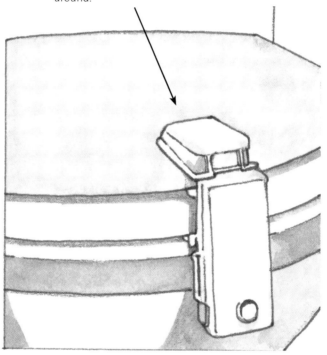

Unfortunately, babies are fascinated with toilets. Aside from the obvious cleanliness issues, parents should be aware that an unattended child could drown in an open toilet.

Transition to the big tub. Around this time, your baby will outgrow her infant tub and graduate to the big bathtub. She might take to the new tub like a fish to water, or she might be afraid of it. To ease her transition and keep her safe, place the infant tub inside the full-size tub for her baths for a week or two.

Unplug the tub. Always empty the water from the bathtub.

Safety Supplies: Inflatable Tub Insert

These inserts fit inside your bathtub, creating a soft, minitub for your baby. You can use these tubs until your baby is around age two. They cost around $10 at baby supplies stores.

BATHTUB SAFETY

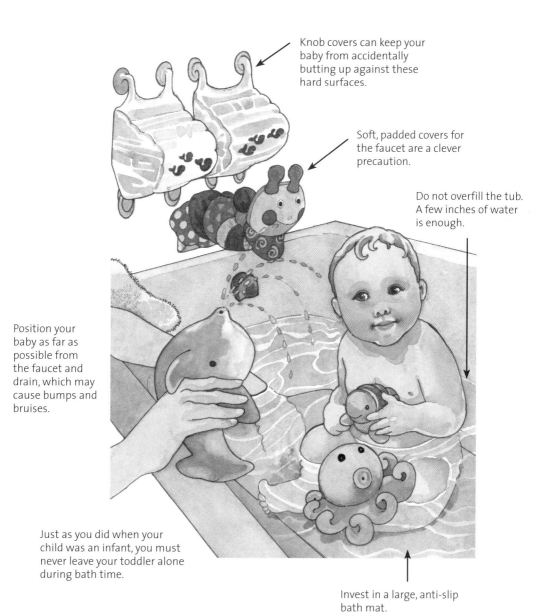

Knob covers can keep your baby from accidentally butting up against these hard surfaces.

Soft, padded covers for the faucet are a clever precaution.

Do not overfill the tub. A few inches of water is enough.

Position your baby as far as possible from the faucet and drain, which may cause bumps and bruises.

Just as you did when your child was an infant, you must never leave your toddler alone during bath time.

Invest in a large, anti-slip bath mat.

Your baby has graduated to the big tub. Always fill the tub before your baby gets in and check the temperature carefully. Keep sharp objects such as razors far away from the tub area. Place a nonslip mat in the bathtub.

Safety Alert: Bathing

Around this time your baby is likely outgrowing her infant tub. Because she is probably able to sit up on her own, you may be transitioning her to an inflatable tub that goes inside your bathtub, or just bathing her inside the bathtub. Chances are your baby has always enjoyed her bath, but now that she can sit up, splash, and play more, she'll probably love bath time even more. Here's how to make it safe:

- Place a nonslip rubber mat in the bathtub. You can buy super long ones for around $20 through baby safety supplies catalogs. A study found that 82 percent of tub injuries are caused by slips and falls.

- Wash the mat frequently to remove the slimy residue that tends to collect on them.

- Because bathing a baby in the tub can be a soggy project, place a thick bath mat on the floor outside the tub. It will soak up extra water and give your baby a sturdy place to stand once she's out of the tub.

- Gather all of your supplies—soap, washcloth, towel, temperature gauge, fresh diaper, and clean clothes—by the tub before you put your baby in. Choose a mild bath soap, one with a neutral pH and minimal dyes and fragrances. A hooded towel is especially helpful to wrap your baby in after her bath.

- At this age, you'll want to have some bath toys, too. Choose age-appropriate toys that are made for the bath.

- Remove any dangers from the tub area, such as shampoo bottles, razors, and scratchy loofas.

- Check the bath water temperature with your wrist or elbow before putting your baby into the water. (Your fingers and palms are not as sensitive to temperature.) It should be warm, not hot—between 96°F and 100°F (35.5°C and 38°C). This is important for safety, but also babies and toddlers generally prefer a much cooler tub than adults.

- Add hot water to cold, never the other way around.
- Turn off the water before putting your baby in. If the water is still running, the temperature could change.
- Turn off the faucets tightly so the water can't drip on your baby.
- Cover the faucets with a washcloth.
- Swirl the water with your hand to make sure there are no hot spots.
- Place your baby in the tub with her back to the faucet and closer to the other end so she can't reach the knobs.
- Use as little soap, shampoo, and bubble bath as possible. They can dry out your baby's skin and cause rashes. Plus bath oils and bubbles can lead to urinary tract infections.
- If you let your baby play in the tub, let her play first, then bathe and shampoo her hair. This reduces the amount of time she'll be sitting in shampoo-filled water, which also can lead to urinary tract infections.
- Whenever a baby is in the bath, an adult must be within arm's length, providing touch supervision, and not distracted by talking on the telephone or with another person, reading a magazine, or doing chores. Never leave a baby unsupervised in the tub for even a second. If you must leave the tub-side for a phone call or to answer the door, wrap your baby in a towel and take her with you. Babies have died when parents left them play unattended in the tub with the water running and the drain open. They assumed the open drain would keep the tub from filling up, but something caused it to clog.
- Never rely on a another child to supervise a baby in a bathtub.
- Teach your child to sit down—not stand up—in the tub. This can take a lot of persistence and reminding.

The Living Room

Now that your baby is more mobile, the living room likely has more appeal. There are fun things to play with, room to explore, and (depending on your opinion on this) TV to watch. Here's how to keep your baby safe.

Take care with plants. Move houseplants out of your baby's reach, and be sure to pick up any leaves that fall to the floor. Know the names of all of your plants in case your baby eats one of them and you have to call poison control. Philodendron, rhododendron, English ivy, lily of the valley, holly, and mistletoe are especially dangerous common houseplants. Plus, leaves and dirt are choking hazards.

Be stable. Shortly after they start crawling, babies usually start pulling themselves up to stand by holding onto furniture. Once your baby starts pulling himself up, inspect your home, paying close attention to the living room, for unstable furniture. If your baby tries to pull himself up on furniture that moves (such as rocking chairs, recliners, or wheeled desk chairs) or that isn't sturdy enough (such as plant stands, blanket racks, or wine racks), the furniture could shift or move, and your baby could go tumbling. Worse, the furniture could come tumbling down on top of him.

Block your baby's access to unstable items as much as possible. (For example, place tall, unstable lamps behind furniture so your baby can't grab for them and pull them over.) Or move the items to another room that your baby doesn't go into.

"When my son, Evan, was starting to crawl, I had the attitude that I didn't want to have to get rid of the decorations I had put around the house," says Marie Suszynski, a mother of one and freelance writer in Emmaus, Pennsylvania. "So for a while I tried to keep an eye on him whenever he went for a floor lamp or my tall candle holders that sit on the floor. But that soon ended because he loved to grab the lamp base and the candle holder base and shake them. I ended up putting the candle holders away, but I probably left the lamp out too long because he eventually broke the top by shaking it too much."

Secure furniture. One study found that dressers, armoires, bookcases, and TV stands often tip over when tested. What looks to you like a chest of drawers looks pretty much like stairs to a baby who can use pulled-out drawers as steps. Use latches on lower drawers and secure furniture to walls with angle braces, anchors, or furniture braces. (See "Safety Supplies: Furniture Braces" on page 130.) Watch your baby at all times around furniture.

Store things carefully. To help prevent furniture from toppling over, put heavier items on lower shelves and in bottom drawers

Remove glass-topped items. Or cover the glass with safety film. Or you could replace the glass with Plexiglas..

Safety Supplies: Furniture Braces

Look for braces that screw into a stud in the wall and then to the furniture. Some of them are made for adults to detach easily to move the furniture to clean underneath. They cost around $6 at baby supplies stores.

Pad sharp edges of coffee tables. You can buy special corner cushions and edge cushions from safety supplies catalogs. Pad the edges of brick or tile fireplaces with cushions made for this purpose out of flame-resistant foam.

"Once my daughter started cruising around in the family room, I was horrified that she might take a nasty fall against the exposed brick edge of our fireplace hearth," says Carol J. Gilmore, a mother of one and freelance editor from Easton, Pennsylvania. "I figured if she was to fall there that it could truly be a nasty scrape, cut, or worse. That's why I was so relieved when I discovered the fire-resistant padded hearth guards that we applied with thick double-sided mounting tape. It didn't look quite as pretty, but it calmed what I felt was a very realistic fear."

Check the TV placement. Make sure your baby can't grab and pull down the TV. An estimated 2,300 children each year are injured by falling TVs, according to the U.S. Consumer Product Safety Commission. TVs are heavy and unstable. Don't place a TV on a cart that could tip over. Place televisions on sturdy furniture as far back as possible. (Or use this as justification for buying that new wall-mounted flat-screen TV.)

Move the remote. "Lots of people keep the remote controls to their televisions on top of the TVs," says John Drengenberg, an electrical engineer and consumer affairs manager for Underwriters Laboratories (UL), a nonprofit product safety certification organization. "A small child could spy the remote and climb up to get it. TVs are very front-heavy, and they can tip over easily. Put your remote someplace else to remove the temptation."

LIVING ROOM SAFETY

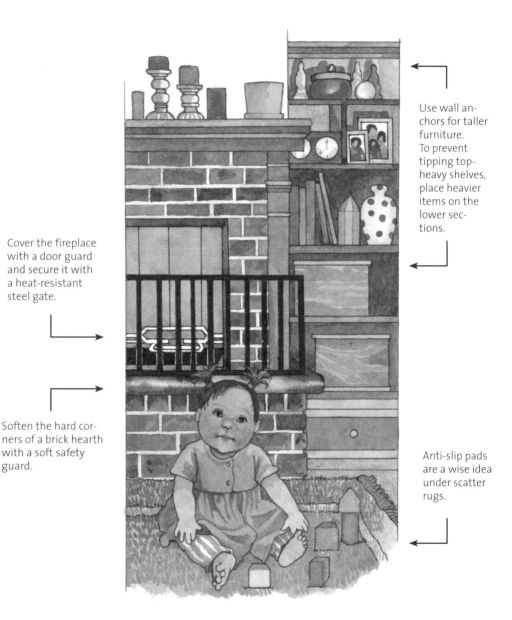

Use wall anchors for taller furniture. To prevent tipping top-heavy shelves, place heavier items on the lower sections.

Cover the fireplace with a door guard and secure it with a heat-resistant steel gate.

Soften the hard corners of a brick hearth with a soft safety guard.

Anti-slip pads are a wise idea under scatter rugs.

Once your baby is mobile, the living room can pose many dangers. From a burning hearth, to a fragile glass-topped table, to a tippy floor lamp, a baby can find all sorts of trouble. Take the time to deal with all the potential hazards so that your family can relax stress-free in this important part of the home.

Safety Supplies: TV Straps

You can buy safety straps that mount to appliances such as TVs and computers to keep them from sliding off the furniture. They mount quickly with heavy-duty adhesive and are easily released with thumb locks. They cost around $15 through baby safety supplies catalogs.

Safety Supplies: TV, VCR, and DVD Guards

To remove some of the temptation of the TV, cover the controls with a plastic cover. You can buy transparent ones that allow you to still use the TV remote.

They make them for VCRs and DVD players as well. They have the advantage of keeping children's fingers—and peanut butter and jelly sandwiches—out of the equipment. They cost about $10 in baby safety supplies catalogs.

Secure rugs. Use nonstick backing on rugs and make sure carpets are tacked down securely.

Move breakables to higher ground. In the flash of an eye, your little crawler could snatch a tchotchke off a coffee table or end table, break it, and then cut himself with the sharp edges or choke on the small pieces.

Potpourri looks and smells an awful lot like food to a baby. Put it away. Also place candles up high or in the center of tables where your baby can't reach them.

Do a safety check. Before placing your baby down to play, do a visual scan for small toys and other choking hazards—such as coins and small barrettes. Babies at this age are expert grabbers, so make sure anything reachable is safe for his hands and mouth, because that's where most things will end up.

"Make sure older children's playthings are out of reach," says Marjorie Hogan, M.D., director of pediatric medical education at the Hennepin County Medical Center in Minneapolis and associate professor of pediatrics at the University of Minnesota. Toys for older children often contain small parts that can be choking hazards to smaller children.

Look out for latex. Balloons are the number one cause of toy deaths. Latex balloons are especially hazardous to kids. A deflated balloon—or part of one—can conform to a child's throat and completely block his breathing. Buy Mylar balloons instead of latex ones. If your baby is given a latex balloon, don't let him chew on it, and when it pops immediately throw the pieces away. Don't let a child under age eight play with balloons unattended.

Similar to latex balloons, pieces of thin latex or rubber gloves, plastic wrap, and plastic bags can conform to a child's throat and block breathing. Don't let your baby play with these types of things.

Beware of batteries. Button batteries, which are in everything from toys to hearing aids, are a choking hazard, plus the electric currents can damage a baby's esophagus if he swallows it.

Keep papers away. Babies love to crumple, fold, and tear paper. But before you give your baby the latest mail-order catalog to shred, consider the habit you're establishing. He can't tell the difference right now between the catalog and your work proposal. Plus, any small piece your baby tears off is likely to go right into his mouth. Fortunately, babies' obsession with tearing paper tends to go away by age two and a half.

Put the play yard sides up. Even if your baby isn't in the play yard, he could try to climb in and get pinched or cut on the unlocked sides.

Remove large toys and bumpers from the play yard. Once your baby is starting to stand, he could use large toys or bumpers as stepping stones to climb out.

Check the play yard rails. If your baby chews on the top rail of his play yard, check the vinyl or fabric for holes and tears. He could pull pieces off and choke.

Pad recliners. If you have recliners, place rolled-up towels between the cushions. If your baby stands up on the recliner cushion, his feet can slip between the cushions and be injured by sharp pieces of the reclining mechanism.

Check into bean bag chairs. Bean bag chairs often contain small, foam pellets that can choke kids. In 1996, manufacturers of the chairs changed the design so kids can't open the zippers.

Secure fish tanks. Make sure the tank isn't accessible to a standing child. A baby is top heavy and can fall headfirst into a tank and not be strong enough to get back out.

Secure fireplaces. Cover your fireplace with a door guard and secure it with a heat-resistant steel gate. Put the key for a gas fireplace in a safe place or consider using a valve cover. These are sold for around $4 on baby safety supplies websites.

Be safe with matches. Teach your baby that matches are tools for adults, not toys for kids. Don't ignite lighters or strike matches in front of children. Store matches and lighters in fire-resistant containers far out of the reach of children.

Move the tools, too. Store fireplace tools out of reach.

Check heaters carefully. If you have space heaters, floor vents, wall heaters, stoves, or other types of things, they can be dangerous for three reasons— temperature, sharp edges, and toppling over.

Here's how to assess their potential dangers: First turn the heater off. Put on gardening or heavy-duty kitchen gloves to protect your fingers. Carefully feel in and around the vents for sharp edges that could cut your baby's fingers. Keep in mind that his small fingers can get into places you wouldn't normally reach.

Next turn the heater on. Carefully get a sense of whether the surface of the heater gets hot enough to burn your child. Keep in mind that a child's skin is more sensitive than an adult's. Then give the heater a shake to see how easily it topples over.

Surround the heater with safety gates. Don't let your baby touch it even when it is cool. He might touch it once safely but get burned the next.

Use space heaters with care. If you're lowering your thermostat to save energy and using a space heater, play it safe. Turn the space heater off when you leave the room or go to sleep. When it's on, make sure it's at least 3 feet (1 m) away from anything that can burn, including people, pets, and furniture. If the space heater gives off smoke, has frayed cords, or smells, replace it.

Store alcohol safely. Don't leave alcohol out where your baby can get his hands on it.

Turn off the shredder. "Unplug the shredder," says Drengenberg. "Babies' fingers are often small enough to fit into the paper opening, and some babies have tried to shred paper, but didn't know to let go of it before their fingers were injured. Some shredders have an automatic feature, where they are activated when paper, or tragically fingers, touch it. Keep your shredder unplugged or better yet, move the shredder to a place where your toddler can't reach it."

Consider upgrading your shredder, says Drengenberg. In 2007, UL will have new requirements for paper shredders, including making the paper opening more difficult for a child's fingers to fit into.

Throughout the House

The words "throughout the house" probably have new meaning for you now. Your baby is likely motoring from object to object and even room to room. Give her plenty of supervised room and time.

Be passive. "I think the hardest babyproofing tasks for parents are those things that need to be done all of the time, such as always turning pot handles to the back of the stove when you're cooking," says Karen Sheehan, M.D., M.P.H., medical director of the Injury Prevention and Research Center at Children's Memorial Hospital in Chicago. "I recommend people babyproof as many of the passive things that need to be done only once, such as turning down your hot water heater or moving breakable vases off of the coffee table. That way you don't have to actively supervise so many things."

Be extra vigilant about small objects. Around eight months of age, your baby will develop a pincher grasp, the ability to pick up an object between her thumb and forefinger. Suddenly, every speck of lint and crumb that were beyond her grasp are grabbable now. Step up your efforts to keep small things out of reach.

With your eyes so far off the ground, it can be difficult to spot things on the floor. But you can bet your crawling baby sees them. Keep an eye out for coins, small balls, rubber bands, rings, pen caps, and millions of other small objects lying on the ground and pick them up immediately.

Look for magnets. Chances are you have several of them in your home and haven't given them a second though. "Magnets are emerging as a danger for young children who might swallow small ones," says Nancy A. Cowles, director of Kids in Danger, a nonprofit organization dedicated to protecting children by improving children's product safety. "If more than one magnet is swallowed, they can connect in the child's intestines and cause a blockage. Don't let children who mouth objects play with magnetic toys and check magnetic building toys often for loose or missing magnets."

Check your shoes at the door. Get into the habit of taking your shoes off when you come inside. That will help keep your floor—where your baby is crawling all over and then putting her hands in her mouth—cleaner, keeping bacteria, dirt, and pesticides outside.

Go HEPA. Consider replacing your vacuum with one with a high-efficiency particulate air (HEPA) filter, which will get your floors cleaner.

Remove the rubber knobs from doorstops. Children can pull them off, put them in their mouths, and choke on them. Or replace the doorstops with one-piece design ones.

My Safety Story

As the sixth born from a family of fourteen, I grew up well aware of how quickly a toddler can get into something potentially hazardous. I thought I had done a very good job of kid-proofing my home. I was wrong.

When my second son, Ryan, was crawling age, I was invited to attend a Tupperware party at a neighbor's house. My sons' father watched the boys.

Behind the doors throughout our home were spring-type doorstops with a little, white, rubber piece on the end of each one. I never thought about how much those white rubber pieces looked like white marshmallows, and I never checked to see if they could come off.

Sometimes we let Ryan have a white marshmallow, and he really liked them. While I was gone, Ryan crawled behind one of those doors and managed to get the rubber piece off the spring and put it into his mouth. His father was too engrossed in his favorite TV show to know what Ryan was doing.

Luckily, our older son, Shawn, age five at the time, was doing a better job of watching his baby brother. He found Ryan choking on the rubber piece, and he quickly got his father's attention. Skip had just learned the Heimlich maneuver in a college first-aid class, and it worked.

When I returned home, Shawn told me all about how he had saved his baby brother's life by getting his father's attention.

—Barbara Sellers, a mother of two in Tacoma, Washington

Install finger pinch guards on doors. This prevents little fingers from being pinched by keeping doors from closing completely. They cost around $2 on baby safety supplies websites.

Go backward. When your baby is ten to twelve months old, teach her to go down stairs backward (facing the steps, like you would descend a ladder). Otherwise, her only example is of you going down forward.

Safety Supplies: Baby Gates

Your baby is likely becoming a real speedster—across the room before you even realize it. Put up gates to keep her out of rooms that aren't completely babyproofed.

At this age, a baby's natural instinct to climb becomes evident. Up is relatively easy, but down is much more difficult. A baby could easily climb to the top of a staircase with no idea of how to get down. Make the stairs off-limits by closing doors or placing safety gates across the top and bottom of all stairways.

Shockingly, almost half of homes with kids under the age of six don't use safety gates on stairs. Once your baby can climb up stairs, she requires either gates or constant supervision.

"When my brother was little, he fell down a flight of steps toward the concrete basement floor. Luckily, our mom wasn't such a good housekeeper, and there was a basket of laundry at the bottom of the steps, which he landed in," says Mary Bright, mother of two and professional crafter in Allentown, Pennsylvania. "With my own kids, I was careful to always keep the door to the basement closed."

Simply put, steps need gates, says Charles Shubin, M.D., director of pediatrics at Mercy FamilyCare in Baltimore, Maryland. Here are some gate specifics:

- Install hardware-mounted safety gates at the top and bottom of stairs.
- Choose gates with a straight top edge and mesh screen and rigid bars or an accordion-style gate with small diamond-shaped openings. Don't use an accordion-style gate with diamond-shaped openings wider than $1\frac{1}{2}$ inches (3.75 cm) between the slats. Children can get their heads caught. Although these gates haven't been sold since 1985, you might find one at a yard sale or in someone's attic.
- Don't use a pressure gate at the top or bottom of stairs because they can pop out of openings. Use hardware-mounted safety gates instead. This goes for any stairway with two or more steps. Falls on stairs tend to cause serious injuries.
- If you use a gate with an expanding pressure bar, install it with the bar away from the child so the child can't use the bar as a toehold to climb over the gate.
- Anchor the gate securely in the doorway.
- Choose gates with safety seals from the Juvenile Products Manufacturers Association.

STAIRCASE SAFETY

Babies this age love to climb, and stairs can become an especially dangerous part of the home. Keep doors to basements closed (even locked) and use secure hardware-mounted gates at the top and bottom of all staircases.

Safety Supplies: Banister Covers

If your home has a second story with banisters, install banister covers. These clear plastic shields, which cost between $20 and $40 depending on length, are available in baby safety supplies catalogs. They attach to your banister with cable ties.

Hide electrical cords. Make cords less visible to crawlers by hiding them behind furniture. And keep things such as lamps unplugged when they're not in use, with the cords tucked out of sight. Keeping appliances close to outlets minimizes the length of exposed electrical cords.

"During his first year, my son, Evan, was obsessed with electrical cords," says Marie Suszynski, a mother of one and freelance writer in Emmaus, Pennsylvania. "One day when he had just started to crawl, I was vacuuming the living room while keeping an eye on him. Evan crawled over to the cord and picked it up. I swooped him up right away because I knew he would have put it into his mouth. From that day on I watched him closely whenever a cord was out, and I bought plastic covers for some of the cords in our house. They got the cords mostly out of sight, and Evan forgot about them."

You can make a jumble of wires coming from stereo and TV equipment less enticing by bundling them together and concealing them inside plastic cord holders. These wire guards cost around $14 for two holders through baby safety supplies catalogs.

Safety Supplies: Power Strip Covers

You can buy plastic covers that snap over an entire power strip. Some include safety plugs to also cover unused outlets on the strip. They cost around $8 through baby safety supplies catalogs.

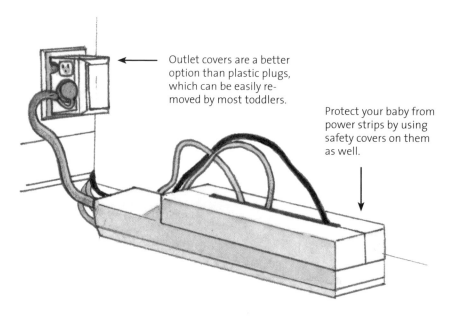

Outlet covers are a better option than plastic plugs, which can be easily removed by most toddlers.

Protect your baby from power strips by using safety covers on them as well.

Babyproofing each and every electrical outlet in your home is an essential task.

Safety Supplies: Electrical Outlet Covers

When your baby sees you plug something in, she'll want to do it, too. This can be disastrous if it's a dangerous appliance or if she tries to plug in a metal object such as a fork. Many young children have been electrocuted that way.

Cover unused outlets. Use child-resistant outlet covers instead of plastic plugs, which are easy to pry out and small enough for a baby to choke on. You can buy self-closing outlets, which you install instead of your outlet face plates. Covers automatically slide over the outlet holes. If you need to plug something in, you just slide the cover to the side. They cost around $4 at baby supplies stores and through baby safety supplies catalogs. If you must use plugs, choose larger-size ones and make sure they fit tightly and aren't easy to remove.

Can it. Open trash cans are invitations to curious babies. Secure cans with latched lids or hide them away in inaccessible locations—such as a locked cabinet or closet. Never line trash cans with plastic bags, because the bags are a suffocation hazard. Move trash out of the house as quickly as possible.

Put paper away. Especially once your baby is standing, paper on desktops is a wonderful temptation: It feels so good to crumple and apparently tastes good to babies, too. To keep your little one from choking on it, keep papers away from the edge of your desk or put them away completely in a basket or drawer once you've finished with them. This will keep your paperwork safe from your baby also.

Move furniture away from windows. To discourage kids from climbing near windows, move furniture away. And keep windows locked.

Keep the key. Make sure you have a way of unlocking any door inside your home from the outside, in case baby toddler locks herself in a room.

Be ready for emergencies. Remember that emergency room file you put together before your baby was born? (See page 29.) Now that her teeth are coming in, add her dentist's phone number to it.

Safety Alert: Guns and Ammunition

The best way to protect your baby from injury and death due to a firearm is to keep your home free of guns and avoid exposing her to homes where guns are kept. Yet the reality is, according to the National Rifle Association, about half of American households have guns. Here's how to make your home as safe as possible. (We'll talk more about toddlers and guns in "Safety Alert: Toddlers and Guns" on page 179.)

- Keep the gun and bullets in separate, inaccessible, locked places.
- Store guns unloaded and uncocked.
- Store guns out of sight of children and visitors.
- Lock up gun-cleaning supplies, which are often poisonous.
- Always use trigger locks or other childproof devices. A trigger lock, which is also called a gun lock, is a vinyl-covered steel cable that you thread through the chamber on a pistol, revolver, or rifle to prevent the firearm's action from closing. They cost about $20 at major retailers. Attach a padlock to revolvers so that the cylinder can't be locked into place.
- Take a firearm safety course to learn the safe and correct way to use your firearm.

Safety Supplies: Window Guards and Stops

A child can fall from windows open as little as 5 inches (13 cm). Yet two-thirds of homes with second and higher floors don't have window guards or locks to keep children from falling out of open windows. Don't depend on screens, which easily pop out of windows.

The type of child statistically most likely to fall from a window is male, under age five, and playing unsupervised at the time of the fall.

To protect your baby from falling from open windows, install window guards. Choose window guards with bars that are 4 inches (10 cm) apart or less and that have emergency releases that are difficult for children to open.

Window guards screw into the side of a window frame. They're sold in different sizes for various size windows. They cost between $50 and $100, depending on the size of the window, in baby safety supplies catalogs.

A simpler, and less expensive, solution is to install window stops. They prevent windows from being opened more than a few inches. This way air can get in, but children can't fall out. They cost around $5 through baby safety supplies catalogs. Some newer windows come with window stops already installed. Or if you have double-hung windows, you can pull the top panes down to let in air, instead of pulling the bottom panes up.

Safety Alert: Introducing Your Baby to Your Dog or Cat

Before now, although your pet was probably acutely interested in your baby, chances are your pet wasn't even a blip on your baby's radar screen. Suddenly, though, your baby has probably taken notice. Children are often so attracted to the family pet that often a baby's first word is the name of her pet. Yet, children one year old and younger are the most likely to be bitten by a dog. Here's how to help your baby get to know your pet safely:

- Consider the dog's breed. A study published in the journal *Pediatrics* found that German Shepherds and Dobermans are more likely to bite children than other breeds—five times more likely than a Labrador retriever or mixed-breed dog. The breeds least likely to bite are spaniels, Shi Tzu, and Maltese.

- Babies are much more likely than older children to aggravate a pet. Teach your baby to be gentle with pets. Don't allow the baby to tug at the pet's tail or poke her eyes. Show your baby how to touch the pet carefully and gently.

- Don't allow your baby to corner, tease, or disturb a pet that's eating, sleeping, or caring for puppies or kittens.
- If at all possible, move your pet's food and water dish to a location where your baby can't reach them. The food is a choking hazard, and the water is a drowning hazard, not to mention unsanitary for your baby to be playing in. Plus your pet won't take kindly to your baby playing near her food.
- Put the cat's litter box in an inaccessible place, too.
- If you have a pet door leading outside, keep it locked. Your curious baby could escape quickly or get stuck in a smaller door.
- Especially now that your baby is probably touching your pet, keep your pet healthy and clean.
- Don't allow your pet to run loose in the woods during poison ivy season. It's possible to get a poison ivy rash from touching a pet that has brushed against the leaves.

Outside

There's so much to do and explore in the great outdoors now that your baby is crawling. Even just playing on soft, green grass is new and exciting to a baby.

Dress carefully. Don't dress your baby in clothes with drawstrings. They could get caught on play equipment or furniture and strangle him. Cut drawstrings out of jackets, hoods, and waistbands. Also, no matter how convenient they are, cut strings off mittens.

Move dangerous substances. Relocate harmful products—such as paint, paint thinner, kerosene, gasoline, charcoal, lighter fluid, bug spray, pesticides, windshield washer fluid, and fertilizers—to upper-level cabinets in the garage and lock them. Always store them in their original containers.

Buy the right antifreeze. Antifreeze looks a lot like a yummy drink and tastes sweet. Buy some that contains denatonium benzoate, which makes it bitter. And store it in a high, locked cabinet.

Stow trash with care. Keep trash cans and recycling bins high or locked up. Your baby could cut himself on something sharp or get sick from drinking substances still left in containers.

Look out for look-alikes. Many household products look a lot like tempting treats to children. In the garage, for example, bleach bottles can resemble milk cartons, and mothballs look like marshmallows. Be especially careful to lock up these look-alikes.

Store tools safely. Keep tools and lawn-care equipment in a locked closet or shed.

Check your garage door opener for safety. "Children don't understand that garage doors are a huge weight that could cause serious injury," says John Drengenberg, an electrical engineer and consumer affairs manager for Underwriters Laboratories, a nonprofit product safety certification organization. "Newer doors have a two-second reverse mechanism. If the door doesn't close completely and make contact with the floor, it immediately reverses. Here's how to test your door. Place a two-by-four under the center of the door and close it. When the door hits the wood, it should reverse automatically."

Another safety feature is electric eyes about a foot off the floor. If these eyes "see" something cross their path—such as a toddler, a dog, or even blowing leaves—when the door is closing, it immediately reverses the door and opens it instead. You can test to make sure yours works by waving your hand in front of the sensor when the door is closing. The door should stop and open back up.

Check old garage door openers. If your garage door opener is more than ten years old, it likely doesn't have the newest safety features, says Drengenberg.

Install gates on your deck. If your deck has stairs, install hardware-mounted gates at the top and bottom, just as you would inside.

"When my son Alex was two, he fell down the stairs of our deck onto a concrete landing pad," says Barbara Bourassa, a mother of two and editor in North Andover, Massachusetts. "He was okay, but it scared the heck out of me! After that I used gates across the top and bottom of all of my stairs."

Inspect slats to ensure that your baby can't squeeze through. Use an extra barrier if needed.

Guard against falls outdoors just as would you would inside. Install hardware-mounted gates at the top and bottom of deck stairs.

Find out if your deck has been built with toxic, pressure-treated wood (see page 152 for more info).

Keep furniture as far away as possible from the edge of the deck so that your baby won't be tempted to climb up and fall over.

Playing on your outdoor deck may pose hazards to your baby beyond mosquito bites and splinters. You must take multiple factors into consideration as you think about outdoor safety.

Add railing guards. If your deck or balcony has horizontal or vertical openings wider than 4 inches (10 cm), install plastic garden fencing, shade cloth, or Plexiglas covers to keep your baby from getting stuck in the openings, falling through them, or climbing up them. Attach the materials with screws or plastic cord ties, but not staples, which can be a choking hazard if they're dislodged.

Keep furniture away. Children can use patio furniture to climb up and over deck and balcony railings. Keep the furniture as far away from railings as possible.

Clear out. Make sure sidewalks and outdoor steps are clear of toys and anything else blocking a clear path.

Keep kids clear. Put your baby inside with another caregiver when you're using a power mower or trimmer. More than 9,000 children are injured in accidents related to lawn mowers each year—hurt by the mower blades or hit by rocks, sticks, or stray toys the blade has thrown. Plus at 90 decibels, the noise can cause hearing loss. Never allow a child to sit on a riding lawn mower either.

Stay away from the grill. Never leave your baby unattended around a grill when you're barbecuing outside. In fact, keep him far away from it.

MY SAFETY STORY

One summer afternoon, I needed something from my yard, and I ran barefoot out onto my wooden deck. Yikes, was it hot. That's when I realized how dangerous it could be for my son, Jacob, to walk or crawl on. Out of curiosity, I took a meat thermometer and laid in on the deck. Within a few seconds, it was up to 140°F [60°C]! That's all the longer my fingers could stand holding it down, but I know it would have gone higher. After that, I was careful not to let my son crawl or walk barefoot on the deck.

—Michael Charles, a father of one and firefighter in Orlando, Florida

CHECKING FOR PRESSURE-TREATED WOOD

Watch out for pressure-treated wood in play structures and decks.

Until recently, virtually all of the lumber sold for outdoor uses in the United States has been pressure-treated with the preservative chromated copper arsenate (CCA) to protect against insects, mold, and weather. It is also known as arsenic-treated or CCA wood. CCA wood has been used for outdoor structures such as benches, decks, fences, gazebos, landscaping timbers, picnic tables, and playground equipment.

"A few years ago, the wood industry began voluntarily phasing arsenic-treated wood out for most residential uses," says Sue Chiang, the pollution prevention program director with the Center for Environmental Health. "But if someone offers you an older play structure, I wouldn't take it. We know arsenic is a carcinogen, and kids should not be exposed to it."

Recent studies have shown that high levels of arsenic can be released to children's hands by direct contact with arsenic-treated wood.

If you think your deck or play structure might be made out of pressure-treated wood, have it tested, says Chiang. You can buy a test kit for $20 at www.safe-2play.org (click on "get a test kit") or call the Safe Playgrounds Project toll-free hotline at 800-652-0827. This simple wipe test will give you an idea of how much arsenic is being released to the wood's surface.

If you have a deck or play structure made out of arsenic-treated wood, replace it if you can, says Chiang. If that's not possible, treat the structure with two coats of solid or semitransparent deck stain at least once a year. Treat high-traffic areas or surfaces—such as handrails, steps, or deck boards—even more frequently. For more details about sealants, check the Safe Playgrounds Project website at www.safe2play.org.

Then be sure to wash your hands—and your baby's hands—after touching it. Keep food off of the wood and use a tablecloth on wooden picnic tables.

Don't store toys or tools under CCA decking exposed to precipitation. Arsenic leaches from the wood when it rains and may coat things left there.

CHECKING YOUR SOIL FOR ARSENIC

Go to www.safe2play.org to order a kit for $20. (Click on "get a test kit.") Research shows that the soil around arsenic-treated wood structures is very often moderately to highly contaminated with arsenic. Don't allow children or pets to play in dirt or sand around arsenic-treated wooden structures or to play on rough wooden surfaces. Avoid eating vegetables grown in proximity to arsenic-treated lumber.

ID plants. Learn about the plants in your yard and keep your baby away from any poisonous ones; better yet, remove them. Knowing the names of them is critical if your baby eats one and you have to call poison control. You can find information about and photos of dozens of common dangerous plants at www.ansci.cornell.edu/plants/alphalist.html, Cornell University's Poisonous Plants Informational Database.

Pull up fungi. As soon as fungi appears in your yard, pull them out.

Steer clear of lawn chemicals. Avoid using any chemicals on your lawn. But if you must treat your grass with fertilizer or pesticides, don't let your baby play on the grass for at least 48 hours, or longer, depending on the manufacturer's instructions.

Paint with care. If you repaint any of your child's outdoor furniture or toys, use only paint labeled "nontoxic."

Safety Supplies: Sunglasses

Exposure to UV rays may increase your baby's risk of cataracts, macular degeneration, and other eye problems later in life. That's why it's a good idea to have him wear sunglasses, if you can. Yet a recent survey found that only 4 percent of parents make sure their children wear sunglasses.

Buy a pair that blocks 99 to 100 percent of both UVA and UVB rays. Look for a label that states "meets ANSI [American National Standards Institute] UV requirements." (You can trust the labels in reliable stores, but not necessarily sunglasses sold by street vendors.)

Choose a pair of sunglasses with medium tint. Lightly tinted lenses don't offer much comfort in bright sunlight, and darker ones will cause your baby's pupils to expand to let in more light, along with more UV radiation.

Be sun safe. Continue to try to keep your baby out of the sun as much as possible. But if that's not possible, use sunscreen. Be sure to cover your child's lips and nose with sunscreen. Even on a cloudy day, 80 percent of UV rays still hit your baby's skin. And the sun has tremendous reflective powers—17 percent on sand and 80 percent on snow. All of these conditions can cause bad burns.

Dress with care. Dress your baby in UV-resistant clothing when he'll be out in the sun for extended periods of time. Clothing has a rating system, similar to the SPF system of sunscreen. UPF, the ultraviolet-protection factor, measures how much ultraviolet light the fabric blocks. For example, UPF 50 means that 1/50th of the UV rays (2 percent) shine through.

Sit still. If your baby suddenly develops an aversion to sitting still in his stroller, try this: Save a few toys that he can play with only in his stroller. Or offer a snack that he doesn't usually get at home.

Do a maintenance check. By now you've probably logged some serious miles on your baby's stroller. It's a good idea to do a safety inspection and some maintenance. Check the stroller for broken or loose parts. Make sure the wheels, brakes, and straps work properly. Check for sharp edges on the stroller. Give the stroller a wipe down, and you're ready to roll.

Dress your baby in UV-resistant clothing when she'll be out in the sun for a while.

Know the plants in your garden. Certain species can be toxic or even deadly if your baby were to ingest them.

Avoid fertilizers. If you must treat your grass with chemicals, don't let your baby play there for at least 48 hours.

When your baby plays outdoors, one concern should be sun safety. However, there are other things to keep in mind, too.

Bug off. Dress your baby in neutral colors, such as white and khaki, to keep annoying insects away. Bright colors and flowered prints are more likely to attract bees and mosquitoes. Plus, it'll be easier to spot ticks and other bugs on light-colored clothes.

Safety Supplies: Bug-Repelling Clothes

L.L. Bean sells the first line of clothing approved by the Environmental Protection Agency that repels insects. The clothing, which is called Buzz Off, has a safe dose of the insecticide permethrin bonded to the fabric. The chemical is an odorless, invisible, man-made version of a natural insect repellent that's found in chrysanthemums. The bug protection lasts for twenty-five washes. At www.llbean.com, two pairs of socks cost around $20, hats around $15, and zip-off pants that convert to shorts around $44.

PART IV

The Toddler Years

FASTER THAN A SPEEDING TRICYCLE! MORE POWERFUL THAN THOMAS THE TANK ENGINE! ABLE TO LEAP TALL PETS IN A SINGLE BOUND! LOOK, OVER THERE IN THE LIVING ROOM, IT'S YOUR TODDLER!

MANY BABIES WALK BY AGE ONE, BUT THAT'S ONLY AN AVERAGE. MANY FACTORS, INCLUDING GENES, HEIGHT, AND WEIGHT, PLAY A ROLE IN THIS DEVELOPMENT. IF YOUR TODDLER IS A FAST CRAWLER, HE MAY BE TOO HAPPY CRAWLING TO HAVE MUCH INCENTIVE TO WALK. ALSO BY THIS TIME (OR EVEN AS EARLY AS TEN MONTHS) TODDLERS MAY BE ABLE TO CLIMB TO THE TOP OF OBJECTS AS HIGH AS A FOOT. PERHAPS YOUR TODDLER CAN EVEN GET BACK DOWN OFF OF A CHAIR BY LOWERING HIMSELF, USING HIS FEET AND LEGS AS FEELERS.

MANY BABY BOOKS SUGGEST THAT IF YOU BABYPROOF YOUR HOME PROPERLY, YOU CAN LET YOUR TODDLER EXPLORE WITHOUT WORRY. IN THE REAL WORLD, HOWEVER, YOU CAN ONLY DO SO MUCH REARRANGING, FENCING OFF, AND LOCKING UP AND STILL HAVE YOUR HOUSE BE A HOME. YOUR TODDLER NEEDS TO LEARN THAT SOME THINGS ARE OFF LIMITS.

AT THIS AGE, PATIENCE, FIRMNESS, AND PERSEVERANCE ARE YOUR WATCHWORDS. YOUR TODDLER NEEDS TO LEARN SELF-CONTROL. BE FIRM, BUT KIND. YOUR TODDLER NEEDS TO LEARN THAT SAFETY ISSUES ARE NOT DEBATABLE. YOUR TODDLER LOOKS FOR CUES FROM YOU ON HOW TO BEHAVE. WHEN HE APPROACHES AN OBJECT, IF YOU'RE SMILING AND RELAXED HE KNOWS IT'S OKAY TO TOUCH IT. IF YOU LOOK UNEASY OR SCARED, HE'LL THINK TWICE.

The Nursery

At this age, your toddler's nursery is in a bit of transition as she graduates from her crib into a bed. This means you need to step up your babyproofing efforts because she might figure out how to get out of her bed or crib at night and wander around unattended.

Move the mattress. By now your toddler's crib mattress should be at its lowest setting. If she is able to climb out, transition her to a toddler bed.

Add some padding. Place a rug under your toddler's crib or bed or place some pillows along the sides. This will provide a bit of cushioning in case of a fall.

Make a safety zone. Take a look at the furniture near your toddler's crib. Can she reach anything on top of it, such as picture frames, her baby monitor, or the lamp?

"Keep any tables near the crib clear," says Jennifer Goldsmith, a mother of one and researcher in Reading, Pennsylvania. "My son, Luke, simply leans over and grabs whatever's on there. Next step, climbing out!"

Look for escape routes. By the time a toddler is eighteen months old, she likely has the physical skills for climbing, but not the understanding of the danger. Having your toddler's dresser next to her crib may have been a great decorating decision, but now that she's more mobile, it might be a stepping stone to help her climb out of her crib. Rearrange the furniture in your toddler's room if need be, keeping other furniture far away from the crib.

Make sure that the mattress is as low as possible now.

If you suspect your baby might attempt an escape from the crib, place something soft on the floor to cushion a potential fall.

Active toddlers love to climb. This will mean stepping up your baby-proofing efforts.

My Safety Story

When my son, Shawn, was about eleven months old, I put him in his crib to take an afternoon nap. I had the ironing board out next to his crib. I didn't have the iron on it, of course, but I had set a big container of baby powder on it. About an hour later, I noticed a strange perfume-like aroma coming from my son's room, so I quickly went to check on him.

It was a sight to behold. Shawn had climbed out of his crib onto the ironing board. He was straddling the ironing board like a horse and shaking the baby powder all over his room. Both Shawn and the deep blue carpet in his room were covered in baby powder! Shawn had a big grin on his face; he was having loads of fun making it "snow" in his room.

This experience taught me an important safety lesson: Never underestimate what a toddler can do. Some of them climb like monkeys.

—Barbara Sellers, a mother of two in Tacoma, Washington

Do a safety check. If your toddler is able to climb out of her crib or bed, do a careful safety check of her room. She might be unattended in there before you realize she's escaped.

Safety Supplies: Crib Tents

Crib tents are mesh coverings that attach to your toddler's crib to keep her from climbing out. They cost around $80 in baby safety supplies catalogs.

"When my son Jack was about a year old, he climbed out of his crib one night," says Barbara Bourassa, a mother of two and editor in North Andover, Massachusetts. "I woke to a big crash and crying. It really scared me, but Jack was fine. We bought a crib tent, which attaches to the top of the crib. You zip it open to get your child in and out."

Graduate to a big-kid bed. Transition your toddler to a toddler bed when she is 35 inches (88 cm) tall. Or you could put the crib mattress on the floor.

Add rails. To keep your toddler from falling out of bed, use detachable bed rails. They cost around $40 each in baby safety supplies catalogs.

Watch for suffocation hazards. Even though your toddler's risk of Sudden Infant Death Syndrome (SIDS) disappears by age one, suffocation is still a danger, and kids' rooms are a danger zone. In 2002, the most recent year for which statistics are available, seventy-five children ages one to five died of suffocation.

Sleep more. Help your toddler get her sleep. Tired children get hurt more often. Preschool-age boys are particularly at risk.

A safety rail is a good idea for children newly out of the crib.

When your child is 35 inches tall, he or she should no longer be sleeping in a crib.

Once your baby is able to climb out of the crib, it's time for a "big kid" bed.

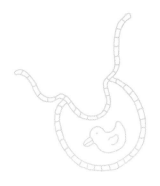

The Kitchen

Because your toddler is more and more mobile—walking, running, climbing—you need to be even more vigilant in the kitchen, which has many potential hazards.

Safety Alert: Feeding

By around a year, toddlers eat almost all table food, cut to pea size. After around a year, your toddler is probably feeding himself, though he won't have mastered the fork and spoon yet. Here's how to keep him safe:

- Always strap your toddler into his high chair to eat. He can swallow better if he's sitting down.
- Check that your toddler's food isn't too hot. Stir and cool food before serving.
- Give your toddler foods that are appropriate for his development. When in doubt, your pediatrician should be a great source of information on this.
- Teach your toddler to chew and swallow his food before drinking, laughing, or talking.
- Continue to be careful about choking. Your toddler's airway is small—not much wider than one of his fingers—and food can prove deadly if it gets stuck. Here are some specifics:
  - Slice hotdogs lengthwise in half, in half again, then into pieces no bigger than 1/4-inch (0.6-cm) wide.
  - Cut grapes into 1/4-inch (0.6-cm) pieces.
  - Chop meat and cheese into very small pieces.
  - Don't give your toddler caramels and chewy candies, dried fruit, gum, hard candies, marshmallows, nuts, popcorn, raisins, raw vegetables, or seeds.

Food Safety

Never serve your
toddler whole
grapes.

Hot dogs can be
a major choking
hazard. Cut them
into small pieces.

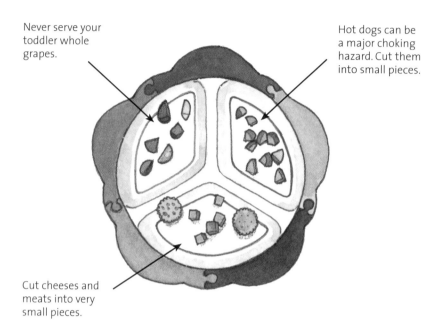

Cut cheeses and
meats into very
small pieces.

Toddlers love to feed themselves with finger foods. Beware of chunky, round, hard, or overly chewy foods, which can all be problematic.

My Safety Story

June 20, 2006, will be a memory forever, and not for good reasons. It was dinnertime, and my ten-month-old son, Tyler, was strapped in his high chair and just finished dinner. We decided to give him his sippy cup to practice. He choked a bit, which is not uncommon with the first few tries of a sippy cup. However, Tyler continued to choke, and I sensed something was terribly wrong. I ripped him out of his high chair and began to give him back blows. Tyler was no longer choking, and the situation became worse. He was not breathing and became unresponsive. I yelled to call 911 and gave back blows again, but Tyler was still unresponsive.

As I continued to hold my son in my arms trying desperately to revive him, thoughts of losing him filled my head and tears filled my eyes. I checked to see if Tyler had a foreign object in his mouth and then gave a chest compression, which caused him to gasp for air and scream. It was music to my ears. Tyler was breathing when the paramedics arrived, and they commented on how quickly I responded and that the situation may have been worse had I not known infant CPR [cardiopulmonary resuscitation].

I suggest that parents and caretakers learn CPR. My mother-in-law watches Tyler from time to time, and we are enrolling her in a CPR course, too.

—Leslie Shotwell, a mother of one and educator in Emmaus, Pennsylvania

Recertify. Now that your toddler is one year old, take another infant CPR and first-aid class. The American Red Cross recommends that parents take a class each year.

Check high chair placement. Keep it away from walls and tables so your toddler can't push off and tip the high chair over.

Enforce this rule. Never allow your toddler to stand up in his high chair.

Extract yourself. Store food extracts, such as vanilla, away from your toddler's reach. They may contain alcohol.

Clear out the sink. If your toddler washes his hands in the sink, keep it clear of dangerous objects such as knives and glasses.

My Safety Story

When my older grandson was about seventeen months old, he took me by the hand into his kitchen and showed me that he could open all of the childproof latches. He had been watching us open them, and he figured out for himself how to do it. He was very proud of his ability to do so. The lesson in this is that anything even potentially dangerous has to be put out of reach.

—Charles Shubin, M.D., director of pediatrics at
Mercy FamilyCare in Baltimore, Maryland

Move 'em back. Keep hot foods and drinks away from the edges of tables and counters so that your toddler can't reach up and knock the food or drink down.

Handle with care. Don't allow your toddler to touch the faucet handles. Even if he can't turn the hot water on now, he'll be strong enough to soon and could easily burn himself.

Teach what's hot. To teach your toddler to stay away from hot things, such as the stove, he needs to learn what hot means. Pull your hand away from something hot and say, "hot!" Then let your toddler feel something warm (but not hot), such as the outside of a coffee mug.

Push chairs in. Push kitchen and dining room chairs in under the tables. They're very tempting for toddlers to climb.

Check out the stove. Once your toddler starts climbing, look closely at the stove and sink. Could he get to them by climbing up shelves or cabinets? Block access to the stove as much as possible.

Make a code. Come up with a signal for your toddler so he knows to keep away from the stove when it is hot. For example, you could turn on the oven fan or light.

Distance yourself. It's critical that your toddler stay away when you're cooking. Yet, it's hard to keep a curious toddler away, especially when he knows your attention is elsewhere. Set your toddler up with an activity that he likes on the far side of the kitchen, where you can still see him. For example, give him a pot, pan, and large wooden spoon so he can pretend to cook, too.

No helping. When you're using cleaning products and other chemicals, keep your toddler away. Don't allow him to help or touch them.

MY SAFETY STORY

I still remember the day my toddler, Kate, drank vinegar thinking it was apple juice. There was a lovely picture of two apples on the label. I thought her eyes were going to pop out of her head! Luckily, she was none the worse for wear.

—Betsy Gammons, a mother of four and
photo editor/project manager in Essex, Massachusetts

The Bathroom

The bathroom continues to be a hazardous place for your toddler, especially because of the water and poisoning dangers. The best practice is still to never leave your toddler alone in a bathroom.

Safety Alert: Bathing

By this age, bathtime is probably an anticipated part of your toddler's day. Here's how to make it safe:

- Whenever a toddler is in the bath, an adult must be within arm's reach, providing touch supervision, and not distracted by talking on the telephone or with another person or doing chores.

- If you're transitioning your toddler to the regular bathtub and haven't done so already, place a nonslip mat in your bathtub to help your toddler get in and out safely.

- A cushioned bathtub spout cover will protect your child's head from painful bumps.

- Face your toddler away from the faucet so she is less likely to play with it or accidentally turn on the hot water. And don't allow her to touch the faucet handles. Even if she can't turn the hot water on now, she'll be strong enough to soon and could easily burn herself.

- Fill the tub so that when your toddler is seated the water comes only to her waist.

- Continue to teach your child to sit down—not stand up—in the tub.

- If your tub has sliding glass shower doors, make sure they're made from safety glass.

- Hold onto your toddler when she's climbing in and out of the tub or, better yet, lift her in and out of the tub yourself.

- When you've finished bathing your toddler, unplug the tub. She might be frightened of the sound at first, but it's best if she gets used to it. You don't want to leave the water sitting in the tub until you have the chance to come back and unplug it.

TODDLER TUB SAFETY

A sitting position is the only safe one in a tub, although children this age often love to jump up. If this happens with your child, firmly tell him, "No standing!"

Water can be filled up to the waist at this age.

Active toddlers definitely need a nonslip surface in the tub.

Never leave your toddler unattended in the bathtub. Stay close enough to provide touch supervision. Steady your toddler when he's entering and exiting the tub, or preferably, lift him in and out yourself.

Don't rely on medicine cabinets. Just because a cabinet is up high doesn't mean your toddler can't get her hands on dangerous things inside. A child will climb up on the toilet and countertops to get into items in the cabinet. Lock the cabinet or, better yet, move the items into an inaccessible, locked closet that your toddler doesn't go in, such as your bedroom closet.

Lock it. If you have a laundry chute, be sure to lock it with a childproof lock.

Go see-through. If your bathroom and surrounding area are very babyproofed and you feel comfortable leaving your toddler play just outside the open door, get a see-through shower curtain. That way you can watch her playing while you take a shower.

Wash up. As you start potty-training your toddler, teach her to always wash her hands after using the bathroom.

My Safety Story

Nonskid mats are very useful in the tub if your child has moved beyond the infant tubs, which typically have a 25-pound [11.5-kg] weight limit—not good for a big toddler!

My son, Jake, likes to stand up in the tub the minute I try to rinse his hair. The mat has saved the day a few times.

—Ruby Guy, a mother of one in Toronto, Ontario, Canada

The Living Room

So much to do, so much to explore. Here's how to keep your toddler safe when he's in the living room.

Clean up. Remove clutter that your walking toddler could trip over. Teach your toddler to put his toys away.

Anchor bookcases. Even if you think they're too heavy to topple over, attach bookcases and other pieces of furniture to walls.

Rearrange. If there are things on bookshelves or furniture that tempt your toddler to climb, move or hide them away

Be a Sherpa. Toddlers love to climb—chairs, furniture, stairs. And like mountaineers, they need a guide to make sure they can get up, and back down, safely. It may be tempting to ban climbing altogether, but your toddler learns important skills and develops coordination by climbing. So be sure to supervise your toddler whenever he's climbing.

Provide safe climbing opportunities. Because your child is going to climb anyway, it's best to provide safe opportunities. You could toss sofa cushions on a carpeted floor, for example..

My Safety Story

You never know what your child will use as a learning-to-stand-and-walk prop. My son, Luke, used our wrought-iron metal CD holder as his pull-up helper once, and it fell and took down a nearby floor lamp with it. Luckily, the CDs just tumbled to the floor, missing Luke, and the CD holder went down at an angle, resting against a chair, with Luke underneath it. Whew!

Luke also liked the diaper pail, an even less steady item, due to the intrigue of its pop-up opening. You always have to be thinking of the unexpected when a toddler's around.

—Jennifer Goldsmith, a mother of one and researcher in Reading, Pennsylvania

Curtail unsafe climbing opportunities. If your toddler is climbing on something unsafe, such as onto the sofa back, take immediate action. Remove him from the perch, make eye contract, and explain to him in a serious tone, "Don't go up there again, or you'll get really hurt."

As your toddler starts to run and climb, he will have many falls and minor accidents. As long as you can see he's not really hurt, give him a quick hug and reassuring smile. Your toddler will take his cue from you. As long as you don't get too upset about the fall, he probably won't either.

Set up a changing station. As your toddler is more and more on the go and less and less patient with diaper changes, it's helpful to set up another diaper-changing station, perhaps in the living room. Stock it with plenty of diapers and wipes so you can change your toddler quickly, before he has the chance to become fussy.

Sit back. If your toddler likes to watch TV standing right in front of it, with his nose pressed to the screen, move him back. Sitting too close can cause focus problems, especially the ability to refocus on objects far away. Put a pillow or kid-size chair about 8 feet (2.5 m) away from the screen and tell him he has to watch TV from there.

My Safety Story

Sometimes when my son, Graydon, heads off into the living room to play, he calls, "Don't worry, Mommy, I'll be careful," over his shoulder. That's when I know I'd better follow him to find out what he's up to.

—Robyn Swatsburg, a mother of two and elementary
school teacher in Biglerville, Pennsylvania

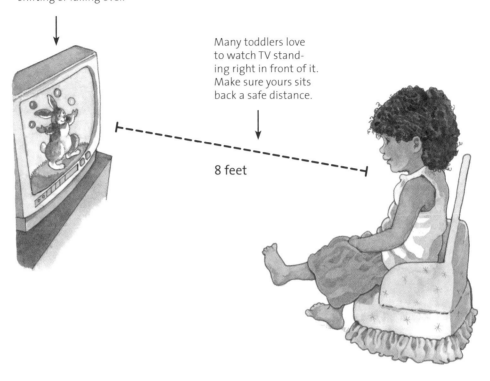

Use an anchoring device to keep your TV from shifting or falling over.

Many toddlers love to watch TV standing right in front of it. Make sure yours sits back a safe distance.

8 feet

Always be aware of what your child is watching on TV. Certain programs can encourage dangerous dare-devil-like pranks.

Watch drinks. Don't leave alcoholic drinks where your toddler can reach them. Take care during parties because guests might leave drinks unattended. Clean up right away after parties.

Color with care. Don't let your toddler put crayons, pencils, or erasers in his mouth when he's coloring. And watch out for broken crayons, which can be a choking hazard.

Unplug. Don't let your toddler toddle around with his pacifier—or anything else—in his mouth.

TiVo it. A service called KidZone from TiVo can help you determine whether a TV show is suitable for your toddler. It includes recommendations from family groups, such as the Parents Television Council.

Throughout the House

Hopefully by now you're feeling really good about the babyproofing state of your home, and you should! Here are just a few more finishing touches throughout your house.

Be positive. "I encourage parents to create a 'yes' environment so that they don't have to tell their children 'no' all of the time," says Marjorie Hogan, M.D., director of pediatric medical education at the Hennepin County Medical Center in Minneapolis and associate professor of pediatrics at the University of Minnesota. "Children need to explore and be curious, and you don't want to stifle that."

"Reserve the word 'no' for true emergencies, such as when your toddler is running headlong into the street," Dr. Hogan adds. "Using the word 'no' is an empty lesson. Save it for when your child is in danger or endangering someone else, such as biting.

"I know parents who say 'no' and 'don't do that' constantly," says Dr. Hogan. "The child starts to tune it out. Instead of saying 'no' all of the time, when you must set a limit, give your toddler two other, positive choices. For example, if your toddler keeps crawling over to the dog's water dish, and it's not possible to move the dish, instead of telling her 'no,' show her a book and a toy to play with instead. Better yet, create a similar, safer opportunity, such as giving her a pan of water to play with supervised instead of the dog's water dish."

Watch out for windows. "Window falls are a serious safety concern," says Karen Sheehan, M.D., M.P.H., medical director of the Injury Prevention and Research Center at Children's Memorial Hospital in Chicago. "Far too often, kids hear an ice cream truck outside, climb up to the top of a sofa to look out, and topple out of a window. People often don't realize that screens are meant to keep bugs out, not kids in."

"Yet window falls can easily be prevented," Dr. Sheehan adds. "First, don't open your windows more than 4 inches [10 cm]. You can buy suction cup window stops, such as Super Stoppers, that attach to your windows and keep them from opening too far. If you need to open your windows farther than that, secure them with releasable childproof window guards. They mount to your window frames, but they are easily released by an adult with emergency release buttons. They can be released from the outside also, for example by a firefighter in the event of a fire."

Go barefoot. Often once babies start walking, parents rush out to buy shoes. But actually toddlers should be barefoot as much as possible indoors. This helps strengthen their foot muscles and ankle muscles and build arches. Feet develop best when they're not confined. Plus when your toddler is barefoot, she can use her foot to grip the floor and develop balance.

Think twice about walkers. According to the U.S. Consumer Product Safety Commission, more kids are injured using walkers—enclosed walking-assistance toys with wheels—than any other nursery product. Toddlers in walkers can fall over objects, roll into pools, and possibly even break through gates. Use a stationary activity center instead. Or consider a push toy, which is also often called a walker.

Bare feet offer new walkers the best stability on surfaces at home.

Push toys are better alternatives to walkers. Few manufacturers even make walkers anymore, since so many child injuries were related to them.

Keep 'em out. Lock doors to rooms that aren't babyproofed. Lock or secure closet doors because they contain many choking and safety hazards.

Keep away from stairs. Never leave your toddler unattended around stairs, even those with gates. She could climb up the gate at the top of the stairs and fall from an even greater height.

Keep heavy items away. It doesn't take a lot of force to break a window, especially older, single-pane windows. Keep hard, heavy objects, such as fireplace tools and bookends, away from your toddler.

Put stickers on glass. Mark sliding glass doors and other big expanses of glass with colorful stickers. Especially if you keep them sparkling clean, your toddler might not see them and go barreling into them.

Safety Alert: Toddlers and Guns

Studies show that guns kill ten to twelve children under age nineteen each day in the United States.

"Gun safety is a critical issue," says Garry Gardner, M.D., a pediatrician in private practice in Darien, Illinois, and former member of the American Academy of Pediatrics Committee on Injury, Violence, and Poison Prevention. "We did a survey in my private practice—a typical, middle-class, suburban community west of Chicago—and discovered that one-third of those homes with children had guns. And some of those guns were loaded and unlocked, 'to keep our homes safe,' the parents say. Those are extremely unsafe homes. The safest home does not have a gun, but if you must have a gun, store it and the ammunition in separate, locked locations."

Here are more ways to keep your toddler safe:

- Start teaching your toddler that guns are weapons, not toys.
- Teach your toddler what to do if she sees a gun. The National Rifle Association's Eddie Eagle GunSafe Program uses these simple rules: Stop. Don't touch. Leave the area. Tell an adult.
- Before your toddler visits another home, ask the parents whether they keep any weapons in the home. If they say yes, ask if the weapons are locked and whether they're loaded. Even if parents keep weapons hidden, children usually know where they are.
- Review the gun safety information in "Safety Alert: Guns and Ammunition" on page 144.

Install banisters. Check that all of the stairs in your home have kid-height banisters. Falls are a leading cause of accidents in kids, yet almost half of homes with children age six or younger don't have handrails or banisters on at least one set of stairs.

Keep clutter free. Make a policy to keep walkways, and especially staircases, clutter free. And fasten down or remove throw rugs. When your toddler is learning to walk, you want to avoid tripping hazards.

Put a rug under stairs. When your toddler starts to learn to go up stairs, place a soft rug at the bottom of the stairs. It will provide a little bit of cushioning if she falls.

My Safety Story

I am very concerned by the cavalier attitude that many people have about guns. I see tragedy caused by guns all of the time. Deer hunters, for example, get up early in the morning and hunt all day, for a week at a time. One father came home from hunting exhausted, leaned his gun up against a wall, and went to sleep. The story ended as tragically as you could imagine. You must be hypervigilant with guns: Store the unloaded gun with a trigger lock in a locked cabinet, and store the ammunition in a separate locked cabinet.

Just like you teach your toddler not to touch knives, light sockets, and fireplace pokers, you need to teach her not to touch guns. You will know when the time is right to begin talking about gun safety. It's usually between the ages of twelve and eighteen months. One day, your toddler will spy something she's not supposed to touch, such as a sharp knife within reach on the kitchen counter. Your toddler will look at the knife, then she'll look at you, then she'll look back at the knife. You'll tell her not to touch the knife, but she'll reach up and grab it anyway. It won't matter if it's a knife, a gun, or a stick of plutonium—she's acting on the human impulse of understanding what the rule is and trying to violate it. That is the day to sit your toddler down and talk about the dangers of guns. That is the day discipline begins.

—Bryan Burke, M.D., general pediatrician and associate professor at the University of Arkansas for Medical Sciences and Arkansas Children's Hospital

Review your fire escape plan. Talk with your toddler about your fire escape plan and have a practice fire drill. Teach your toddler how to escape from a fire, not to hide under a bed or in a closet.

"Teach your children that it's safe to go outdoors if the smoke alarm goes off," says John Drengenberg, an electrical engineer and consumer affairs manager for Underwriters Laboratories (UL), a nonprofit product safety certification organization. "Some parents, with good intentions, teach their kids not to go outside after dark, for example. But the children might not understand that they should go outside after dark if the smoke alarm goes off."

Also, teach your toddler to stop, drop, and roll if her clothing catches fire.

Safety Supplies: Door Knob Covers and Overhead Door Latches

If you want to keep your toddler out of a room that you can't keep locked, such as the powder room, try plastic door knob covers. They snap right over door knobs. Adults can still turn the knob by pressing in two buttons, but toddlers shouldn't be able to open them. They cost around $4 at baby supplies stores and through baby safety supplies catalogs.

Plastic door knob covers work great on round door knobs. However, they're useless for lever door handles, which are common in newer homes. To make those doors inaccessible to toddlers, install overhead door latches. You can buy them at baby safety supplies websites for around $7. Unfortunately, they'll also keep out older kids and short adults who can't reach the top of the door to move the latch!

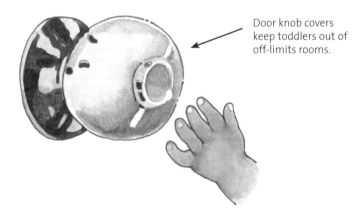

Door knob covers keep toddlers out of off-limits rooms.

Use door knob covers to close off doors to dangerous stairwells or places containing serious hazards, such as a workshop. In these cases, it is vital to keep your roaming toddler safely out.

Safety Alert: Keeping Your Dog or Cat and Toddler Safe from Each Other

Now that your toddler is more mobile and independent, she's bound to have more interaction with the family pet. And that's not a bad thing; pets are fun for kids to be around, and they help kids learn about nurturing, companionship, and responsibility. Yet there's always a danger, around dogs especially. Each year about 400,000 kids need medical attention for dog bites, and 80 percent of dog bites are from dogs that the children know. According to a study in the journal *Pediatrics*, one-year-olds are most vulnerable. Here's how to help your toddler interact with pets safely:

- Teach your toddler not to bother a pet that's eating, sleeping, or caring for puppies or kittens.

- Show your toddler to stroke a pet's back and sides, but not to reach toward or over her head or pick her up.

- Teach your toddler not to behave aggressively toward a pet, such as screaming or lunging at it.

- Any pet can have a bad day. Teach your toddler how to recognize your pet's moods.

- Keep your toddler away from the pet's poop.

- Take your pet to the vet for regular checkups.

- Teach your child to stay away from stray or outdoor pets. They might be carrying diseases and parasites.

- If your child encounters an unfamiliar dog, teach her to stand still with her hands at her sides ("be a tree") and let the dog sniff her. Explain that if she runs away, the dog might think she's playing and chase her. Along the same lines, teach her never to run past a dog.

- Teach you toddler to avoid dogs that are growling, baring teeth, or whose fur is standing on end. Generally, cats run away if they're bothered by a child. But teach your toddler that if a cat flips its tail back and forth quickly, it's upset and must be avoided.

Safety Alert: Keeping Your Dog or Cat and Toddler Safe from Each Other (continued)

- Tell your toddler never to stare into a dog's eyes, which can antagonize it.

- Teach your toddler to see if a dog is with an owner and looks friendly. Before approaching the dog, ask the owner for permission. Let the dog sniff your child, and have your child touch the dog gently, avoiding the face, head, and tail.

- Teach your child that if she is knocked down by a dog, she should curl into a ball and protect her face with her hands.

Teach your child not to approach or antagonize animals. When encountering a new animal, the child should "be a tree" as shown above. If the child runs away, the dog might think she's playing and chase her.

Outside

Running, jumping, playing—now's when the fun outside really begins! Even though your toddler is doing many new things, his safety is still a huge responsibility for you. He doesn't know what his limits are.

Secure doors. Make sure your toddler can't get outside of the house by himself. Put door knob covers on exterior doors or install childproof locks. (See "Safety Supplies: Door Knob Covers and Overhead Door Latches" on page 181.)

Lock outside doors and windows. Especially if you have a outdoor pool, hot tub, or landscape pond, lock all doors and windows that lead outside. Make sure the latches are out of your toddler's reach and use them at all times. Ask houseguests to latch the doors as well.

Make your alarm do double-duty. If you have a security alarm system, check if it has a chime feature. With this feature, the system will chime if outside doors or windows are opened.

My Safety Story

When my twin boys were toddlers, we lived on a busy street, and our house stuck out into the road further than the rest. One day, my mother was visiting, and we were taking things from the house to her car. We didn't notice that the boys had slipped out until we saw them sitting by themselves next to the mailbox, right by the street!

After that, we were much more aware of when the boys were outside. Also we were careful to always use the keyed deadbolt on the front door. We always lock ourselves in, and even at nine years old, the boys can't turn the key themselves.

—Susan Schlack, a mother of twins in Bethlehem, Pennsylvania

Buy the right shoe. Barefoot is best for indoors, but when your toddler will be walking outside or if the walking surface is hot, cold, unsafe, or unsanitary, he needs shoes. The shoes you choose should be like your toddler's bare feet: soft and flexible, with plenty of movement. Look for shoes that have these attributes. They will help your toddler's foot grip the ground more easily than hard-soled shoes. Your toddler's feet will breathe best in leather, cloth, or canvas. The shoes should be low-cut; high-tops are too confining. The bottoms should be nonskid.

Choose sandals with care. Toddlers need flexible, but firm, sandals for their developing foot muscles and arches. Sports sandals are usually the best choice. Forget open-backed sandals such as flip-flops. Back straps will keep your toddler's feet from sliding out when he's running. Look for a flexible sole. When you flex the shoe, it should bend easily at the ball of the foot (right below the toes), not in the middle. And it shouldn't twist like a pretzel.

Stay cool. Kids under the age of five are especially vulnerable to heat illness. If the heat index is above 100°F (38°C), don't let your toddler play outside for more than 30 to 60 minutes at a time. And dress him in loose, breathable fabrics, such as cotton.

Slather up. Now that your toddler is older and more active, the keep-him-in-the-shade technique is less likely to work. Yet, if a child gets just one bad sunburn, his chance of getting melanoma—the most deadly form of skin cancer—doubles. Melanoma now strikes kids as young as ten.

Use a sunscreen with an SPF (sun-protection factor) of at least 30 that protects against UVA and UVB rays. (If you use an SPF 30 product, in theory you should be able to stay in the sun 30 times longer than if your skin were bare. In actuality, however, sunscreen washes, wears, and rubs off.) Put sunscreen on your toddler's exposed skin about 20 minutes before you go outdoors to give his skin time to absorb the lotion.

Because the average white T-shirt has only an SPF of 3, apply sunscreen under your toddler's clothes, too. Plus, if you put sunscreen on before he gets dressed, you're less likely to miss a spot. Common spots to miss are the ears, nape of the neck, chin, tops of the feet, backs of the hands, and part in the hair.

Darker-skinned children have more natural protection because of the melanin in their skin, but it's only the equivalent of an SPF 8.

Use enough. Don't spare the sunscreen. You should use about an ounce of lotion (enough to fill a shot glass) to cover your toddler. Don't get a false sense of security. It's easy for a parent to think that because a toddler has sunscreen on, he's protected for hours. Consequently, kids may be spending even more time in the sun, exposed to even more UV radiation.

If your toddler is getting a tan line, you need to do more to block the rays. Another clue? If your sunscreen expires before you use it up. It lasts only about three years, and most have expiration dates on them. But if you're applying enough, you should use several bottles in a season.

SUN SAFETY

Put sunscreen on 20 minutes before heading outdoors, and reapply often.

A sun visor or sunglasses are recommended to protect your toddler's eyes.

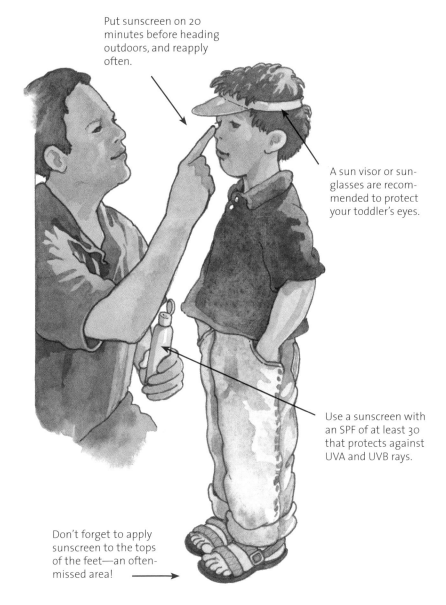

Use a sunscreen with an SPF of at least 30 that protects against UVA and UVB rays.

Don't forget to apply sunscreen to the tops of the feet—an often-missed area!

Unlike earlier stages, it is no longer realistic to expect your active child to stay planted in the shade. Now, more than ever, you will need to guard against the sun's damaging rays. Bear in mind that just one bad childhood sunburn doubles a person's chances of getting melanoma down the road.

Safety Supplies: SunSignals UV Sensors

Need a reminder to reapply your toddler's sunscreen? Put SunSignals UV Sensors on your toddler, where they absorb the sun's rays. When the stickers change color, it's time to reapply sunscreen or head indoors.

SunSignals cost around $7 through baby safety supplies catalogs.

Skip this. Don't use combination sunscreen/DEET products. Sunscreen needs to be reapplied often, but DEET does not.

Inspect toys. Regularly check your child's outdoor toys for sharp edges, splinters, weak seams, rust, or broken parts. Repair any that you can and discard any that you can't. Sand any sharp or splintered surfaces on wooden toys.

Keep away. The best way to protect your toddler from bees, hornets, wasps, and fire ants is to teach him not to swat at them or disturb their nests. Teach your toddler that if insects are swarming around him, he needs to stand still and cover his face.

Safety Supplies: Laundry Treatment UV Protectant

Rit SunGuard makes this product, which increases the sun-protectiveness of clothing. You can buy it for around $20 at major retailers.

✎ *Using safety signs, such as the Sidewalk Sammy, near your home helps alert drivers that children are at play.*

Safety Supplies: Sidewalk Sammy

You can purchase signs to alert motorists that kids are at play. One especially creative sign is called Sidewalk Sammy. It's a childlike figure that stands 32 inches (81 cm) tall and holds a 39-inch (99-cm)-tall red warning flag. It requires minimal assembly. Order one at www.childsafety.com or 800-709-SAFE.

The company also sells A-frame signs that state "Be Alert for Children" and "Slow—Kids at Play."

Display the signs only when children really are at play. If the signs are out all of the time, they become less noticeable.

Teach street safety. Instruct your toddler to be wary of cars and to hold a grown-up's hand in parking lots and around streets.

"My son, Evan, is active and loves to go outside and walk around the block," says Marie Suszynski, a mother of one and freelance writer in Emmaus, Pennsylvania. "When we first started walking outside, I tried to get him to hold my hand, but he would shake it loose or use his other hand to pull it off. He wants to be so independent! So I set a rule that he has to hold my hand when we cross the street, but he can walk on his own on the sidewalk. At first Evan resisted and every time he did I picked him up and carried him across the street. He eventually learned the rule and now holds my hand in the street and quickly drops it when we get to the sidewalk."

Keep kids away from cars. Don't let your toddler—in fact any kid under age ten—cross streets alone, and don't let kids play in driveways, parking lots, streets, and unfenced yards near streets.

My Safety Story

The first word most babies learn to understand is "no." But I believe the first word you should teach your child is actually "stop." More important than "no," the word "stop" is critical if you need to keep a little one from running into the street, as I did one heart-stopping moment.

—Tori Dennis, a mother of three in Tuscumbia, Alabama

Safety Supplies: *Keep Kids Alive* Drive 25

Visit the website www.keepkidsalivedrive25.org for information about starting a campaign to slow down drivers in your neighborhood. The website sells yard signs, street signs, trash can decals, and more with the *Keep Kids Alive* Drive 25 logo.

A study in Oceanside, California, showed that drivers slowed down an average of 16 percent in neighborhoods with *Keep Kids Alive* Drive 25 signs in yards. Another study showed that 75 percent of drivers who drive past the signs apply their brakes.

Safety Supplies: Driveway Guards

It's best for kids never to play in driveways. But if it's unavoidable, a driveway guard can create a visible barrier between your kids and traffic, keeping cars out and kids and toys in. They cost around $80 at home improvement centers.

Cover the sandbox. This will prevent animals from fouling it.

Do doo-doo patrol. Don't allow pets to defecate in the yard, or at least clean it up promptly.

Empty containers. After each use, pour all of the water out of baby pools, car-washing buckets, or any other containers filled with water. Then turn them upside down. Containers can collect rainwater, and top-heavy toddlers can fall in and drown. Never leave a container containing water unattended.

Block access. Because they often contain fish and fountains, landscape ponds are toddler-magnets. Block access or, better yet, drain them.

Installing a Pool Fence

Having a pool or hot tub is a major responsibility. According to the U.S. Consumer Product Safety Commission, 250 children under age five drown each year in swimming pools. Kids ages four and under are two to three times more likely to drown than any other age group. There is rarely a splash or cry to alert caregivers to a baby's drowning. The most common drowning victim is a boy one to three years old who is thought not to be in the pool area.

"Have as many lines of defense for pool safety as you can," says John Drengenberg, an electrical engineer and consumer affairs manager for Underwriters Laboratories (UL), a nonprofit product safety certification organization.

If you have a swimming pool or hot tub—anything larger than a kiddie wading pool, including inflatable pools, you need a fence. According to the American Academy of Pediatrics, having an isolation fence (one that surrounds the water on all four sides, is at least 4 feet [1.25 m] high, and is tough to climb) can prevent more than half of pool drownings. Install a fence at least 4 feet (1.25 m) tall (higher if required by local ordinance) around the pool with self-closing and -latching gates. It can cost as little as $5 per linear foot. The latches should be out of a child's reach.

Avoid fences with easy toeholds for children to climb, such as chain link fences. Make sure the fence isn't more than 4 inches (10 cm) off the ground so a toddler can't slip beneath it and that the distance between slats is less than 4 inches (10 cm) as well.

The gate should swing open away from the pool. Check it often to make sure it latches properly. Never prop open a gate to the pool area.

Keep furniture that a child could use to climb over the gate away from the fence.

If your house forms one side of the barrier to the pool, install alarms that sound when the doors are opened on doors leading from the house to the pool.

Appoint a designated watcher. Never leave a child unsupervised near water for even a second. Nine out of ten children who drown were not under some sort of supervision. And 60 percent of drowning victims are under age four.

No matter what kind of safety devices you have for your hot tub, pond, or pool, never let a child go near the water for even a second without 100 percent adult supervision. During social gatherings near pools, make sure at least one adult is 100 percent focused on children playing in and around the water.

Whenever a toddler is near water, an adult must be within arm's length, providing touch supervision, and not distracted by talking on the telephone or with another person or doing chores.

"Follow the 10/20 rule around pools," says John Drengenberg, an electrical engineer and consumer affairs manager for Underwriters Laboratories (UL), a nonprofit product safety certification organization. "If there are children in your pool, scan the pool every 10 seconds and make sure that you are close enough to the pool that you could be in it in 20 seconds in case of an emergency."

Always have a phone accessible poolside. Either bring your cell phone or cordless phone. (Make sure you're still in range!) Post emergency numbers by the pool if they're not programmed into the phone.

Keep rescue equipment at the ready. Air-filled swimming aids such as water wings are not life preservers. Buy equipment approved by the U. S. Coast Guard, including life preservers, life jackets, and shepherd's crooks.

Lock up the ladder. Be sure to remove or secure the ladder for above-ground pools when they aren't in use.

Don't leave toys in the water. Remove pool toys and floats from your pool promptly because they might attract young children to the water. Don't use pool chemical dispensers that look like toys. And never treat pool toys like flotation aids.

Keep nonpool toys far from water. Kids can fall into the water easily when reaching for toys or riding on toys such as tricycles.

Stop. Don't allow your toddler to run or play near the pool. No pushing or jumping on each other in the pool either.

Hold off on swimming lessons. Children aren't developmentally ready for formal lessons until after age four. Plus, a toddler who likes and is used to water is probably less safe near it than one who is less comfortable with, or even fearful of it.

Pool Safety

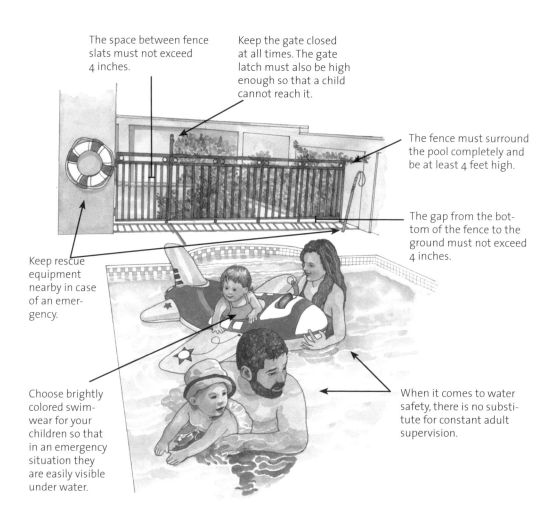

The space between fence slats must not exceed 4 inches.

Keep the gate closed at all times. The gate latch must also be high enough so that a child cannot reach it.

The fence must surround the pool completely and be at least 4 feet high.

The gap from the bottom of the fence to the ground must not exceed 4 inches.

Keep rescue equipment nearby in case of an emergency.

Choose brightly colored swimwear for your children so that in an emergency situation they are easily visible under water.

When it comes to water safety, there is no substitute for constant adult supervision.

Pool safety is no small matter. If you own a pool, you should have several lines of defense against accidental drownings, including isolation fences, gate locks, alarms, and handy rescue equipment. Vigilant supervision is critical.

Safety Supplies: Motorized Pool Covers

A motorized safety cover, while not a substitute for a fence—can provide a barrier over the water when the pool isn't in use. Use it even during swimming season. The cover must be strong enough to support two adults and a child in case a rescue is needed.

They don't come cheap—around $1,000 for an average-size pool.

Look in the pool first. Know where your toddler is at all times. But if a child is missing, check the pool immediately. Drowning can happen in 3 minutes. Nearly 70 percent of children who drowned were not expected to have been near the pool when they were found in the water.

Go bright. Buy a bright, multi-colored swimsuit for your toddler. If he slips under the water, he might be harder to see in a light, one-color suit.

Cover spas and hot tubs. Always secure safety covers and barriers, such as gates. Solar covers and other nonrigid covers can appear to be in place even after children slip underneath them into the water.

Watch out for standing water. If you use a pool cover, don't let water collect on top of it. Even a small amount of water can be a drowning hazard.

Stay clear of drains. Children can get sucked down and trapped in a pool or hot tub drain. Or their hair or bathing suits can get stuck. The suction can be so powerful that even adults can't pull them free.

Make sure your toddler doesn't go near the drains, tie girls' hair back, and make sure swimsuits fit snugly with no loose ties. Be sure that any pool or hot tub has anti-entrapment drain covers. Pools and hot tubs should have at least two drains for each pump, which will reduce the powerful suction if one drain is blocked.

Safety Supplies: Pool Alarms

Choose an alarm that meets the American Society for Testing and Materials (ASTM) standard. Check to make sure the alarm can be heard inside the house and in other places away from the pool area.

The most reliable alarms are designed to detect movement under water. They cost around $200 at pool supplies stores. Surface devices that detect waves are helpful, but they're more likely to give false alarms. Also, they can't be used when a pool cover is in place. .

Heed the leaves of three. If your toddler is going to be running around outside, keep an eye out for poison ivy (and oak and sumac). If your toddler might have come into contact with the plants, wash his skin immediately with soap and cold water. (This might prevent a rash if you washing within 15 to 30 minutes of contact.) To prevent spreading the urushiol—the plant's rash-causing oil—try to keep his clothing from touching your hands, the car upholstery, and furniture, if possible, and machine-wash it.

Stay warm. In cold weather, don't keep your toddler outside for more than 20 to 30 minutes when the temperature is below freezing. Children are especially susceptible to frostbite because they lose heat rapidly from their skin, and they often ignore mild discomfort so they can continue playing. When the temperature is below freezing and has a wind chill factor, frostbite can occur in less than an hour. Change clothes that become wet from sweat or snow.

Be wise, supervise. According to a study conducted by the National Center for Missing & Exploited Children, 49 percent of people believe their neighborhoods are so safe that they are not concerned about their children going missing. However, in the majority of child victimization cases, the perpetrator is someone a parent or child knows. Keep an eye on your toddler always, even if he is right in your backyard.

Safety Supplies: Safety Turtles

With this safety system, you attach a wristband around your toddler's wrist. Then you place the alarm base station within 100 feet (30.5 m) of the water. If the child enters the water, the alarm base station sounds.

This system works around any kind of fresh water, such as a pool, hot tub, lake, or river. You can't use it in seawater, however.

Safety Turtles alarm base stations cost around $110, and the wristbands cost around $49 at pool supplies stores.

PART V

Out and About

So much about parenting is a balancing act. You want your child to be safe, yet she needs to explore. Although you might sometimes yearn to keep your child right next to you every second to protect her from harm, you know that touching, holding, climbing, and exploring are the activities that develop a child's body and mind. You've done your best to make your home a safe haven. Yet you know that the rest of the world is out of your control.

This part of the book isn't age specific. Instead it talks about both babies and toddlers. Here's how to help your little one stay safe as you venture out and about.

In the Car

"Motor vehicle crashes are the leading cause of death for children ages three to fourteen," says Alexander Sinclair, a highway safety specialist with the National Highway Traffic Safety Administration (NHTSA). This includes crashes with kids as passengers in cars as well as bicycle crashes and pedestrian crashes.

Most car crashes occur between 10 a.m. and 4 p.m., and 5 to 10 minutes from home, according to a study by researchers at the Children's Hospital of Philadelphia.

Set a good example. "Make sure that everyone in your car wears their seat belts," says Bryan Burke, M.D., general pediatrician and associate professor at the University of Arkansas for Medical Sciences and Arkansas Children's Hospital. "Especially when my children are in the car, I insist that other people wear their seat belts as well. I wouldn't want my kids to think that it's acceptable to not wear your seat belt."

Be seated. "Half of the kids who die in crashes are unrestrained," says Sinclair. "Yet, the older children get, the less likely they are to be properly restrained: 98 percent of infants under age one are restrained, but for toddlers between one and four, that drops to 89 percent, and for kids ages four to eight it drops to 76 percent. That means one in four of those kids is riding in a car unrestrained."

Different types of seats are designed for different weight, and ages, of kids. Here's the progression.

"As a child gets older, just like her education goes through stages, her safety in motor vehicles goes through stages as well," says Sinclair. "We call it the '4 Steps for Kids Program.' Here's how the progression works. Babies ride in rear-facing infant car seats from birth until they are one year and 20 pounds [9 kg]. From age one and 20 pounds [9 kg] to about age four and 40 pounds [18 kg] , they should ride in a forward-facing car seat. When children outgrow forward-facing child safety seats, they need to be restrained in belt-positioning booster seats. This usually occurs when children are about four years old and weigh approximately 40 pounds [18 kg] . To ensure children's safety, they should remain in booster seats until they are at least eight years old, unless they are 4 feet 9 inches [1.5 m] tall. Then they graduate to the regular car seat belts. All children age twelve and under should always ride in the backseat.

"It might help parents to insist their older child ride in her car seat or booster seat by getting her involved in choosing the seat," continues Sinclair. "You could let her help you decide which car seat to buy, for instance to choose between a grey and a blue seat or to pick one with a cup holder."

Read up on it. Always install your car seat in accordance with the car's and car seat's manufacturer's recommendations. Your car's manual should contain information about installing a seat safely in your particular vehicle. If the instructions aren't clear, call the manfuacturer to ask for more help.

CHOOSING THE SAFEST CAR SEAT

"Parents must insist their kids be secured in motor vehicles," says Alexander Sinclair, a highway safety specialist with the National Highway Traffic Safety Administration (NHTSA). "Some things must be nonnegotiable. Yet a lot of parents make compromises as kids get older. It can be difficult for parents to be firm, but you must be firm on this point."

According to Safe Kids USA, a correctly installed car seat reduces the risk of a baby dying in a car crash by 71 percent. However it's estimated that 82 percent of children are improperly restrained.

According to the NHTSA, the best car seat is the one that fits your child, that you can securely install in the backseat of your vehicle, and that you will use on every single trip. Here are some more specifics:

- Purchase a new seat. A used one may be weakened from previous use. Car seats expire after eight to ten years. According to Kids In Danger, an organization dedicated to improving children's product safety, car seats more than five years old are too old to reuse.

- Never buy a car seat at a yard sale or secondhand store because it may have been involved in a crash.

- If you must use a secondhand seat, call the NHTSA's hotline for recall information at 888-327-4236. Make sure the seat doesn't have any cracks in the frame. If it didn't come with instructions, get a copy from the manufacturer. Make sure the car seat has all of its parts.

- "When choosing a car seat, check out the NHTSA's Ease of Use Ratings," says Sinclair. In 2006, they evaluated ninety-nine car seats from fourteen manufacturers. You can find the results at www.nhtsa.gov; search on "ease of use ratings." Seats are graded A, B, and C for such things as ease of assembly, use, and securing the child.

"When choosing a car seat, know that all seats must meet federal standards, so one seat really isn't safer than another," says Sinclair. The differences you see are mainly colors, brands, and features such as cup holders.

- Look for a U.S. Department of Transportation label that states, "This child-restraint system conforms to all applicable federal motor-safety standards."

- There are so many different models of cars and so many different models of car seats that not all of the car seats are good fits for all of the cars. If you happen to be in the market for a new car, take your car seat to the showroom and install it to check fit.

"Before you purchase a car seat, ask the store if you can test the seat out in your car before you buy it," says Sinclair. "If you're not able to install the car seat securely, take it back."

- Put your child in the seat and test it. Adjust the harnesses and buckles. Make sure it fits properly and securely in your car.

- Choose a seat with a five-point harness.

- Look for seats that come with more than one harness slot and buckle position to give your baby room to grow.

- Angle indicators, which come on some car seats, can help you get the proper recline.

CAR SEAT SAFETY

Choose a seat with a
5-point harness.

Infants ride in rear-facing
car seats from birth until
they are one year *and*
twenty pounds.

Never place a car seat
in the front of a vehicle.
The rear, center position
is the safest.

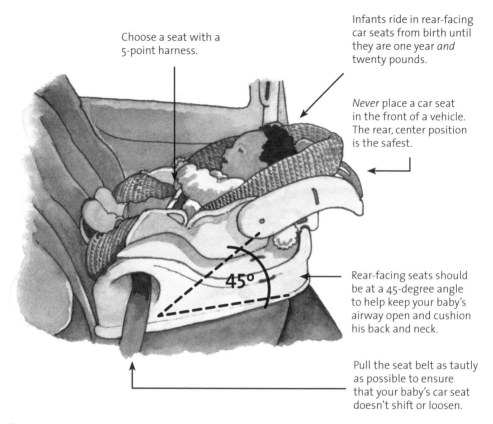

45°

Rear-facing seats should
be at a 45-degree angle
to help keep your baby's
airway open and cushion
his back and neck.

Pull the seat belt as tautly
as possible to ensure
that your baby's car seat
doesn't shift or loosen.

*Selecting the appropriate car seat for your child, and using it correctly, might
very well save his life in an automobile accident. Take your time choosing the
seat, installing it, and properly securing your child for each and every trip.*

Sit back. Babies are 30 percent more likely to survive a crash if they're in the
backseat. Babies should never ride in the front seat of a car with a passenger-
side airbag. All new cars come equipped with air bags, which do a tremendous
job of protecting adults in car crashes. But even in a low-speed crash, the air
bag can inflate—at speeds up to 200 miles per hour—strike the safety seat,
and cause serious brain and neck injury and death. In fact, all children under
age twelve are safest in the backseat.

Learn about LATCH. Lower Anchors and Tethers for Children (LATCH) is an attachment system that makes installing car seats easier. Instead of using the car's seat belts, you use two sets of small bars, called anchors, that are located in the backseat where the seat and back cushions meet. Nearly all cars made after September 1, 2002, come with LATCH. All safety seats made after that date come with a set of attachments that fasten to those vehicle anchors.

"It takes about 20 to 30 minutes to install a car seat correctly," says Sinclair. "LATCH is designed to make the car seat easier to install, not necessarily safer. We'd like to reassure parents that you can install a car seat perfectly well with seat belts. This is important because most cars on the road today are not LATCH-equipped, since the LATCH system only became mandatory in 2002."

Lower Anchors and Tethers for Children (LATCH) is an attachment system that makes installing car seats easier. Now, instead of trying to secure your car seat with the car's seat belts, you can strap it to the top tether anchor and lower, side anchorage points in your vehicle (most newer vehicles have these). Newer safety seats also come equipped to adapt to the LATCH system.

Pick one. "Don't use both LATCH and your car's seat belt to install your child's car seat, unless the automaker and car seat manufacturer specifically permit it," says Sinclair. "The reason is because the car seat hasn't been tested that way, so no one knows if it will work properly, and you should always use your car seat in accordance with the manufacturer's instructions."

Some car seats are safer if attached with seat belts instead of LATCH. Check with your seat's manufacturer. Use seat belts instead of LATCH if your child weighs more than 47 pounds (21 kg).

Be safer with tethers. A tether is different from the LATCH attachments. A tether is a long strap that attaches at the top of a forward-facing car safety seat to an anchor located on your car's rear window ledge, back of the vehicle seat, or on the floor or ceiling of the vehicle. Tethers keep the car safety seat and the child's head from moving too far forward in a crash or stop. All new cars, minivans, and light trucks have been required to have tether anchors since September 2000. Most new forward-facing car seats, and a few rear-facing ones, come with tethers. Tether kits are available for older car seats. Check with the manufacturer to find out how to get a tether for your seat if it didn't come with one.

Center. If recommended by your car's and car seat's manufacturers, install the car seat in the center rear seat, where it's farthest from any possible impact from any direction. If LATCH attachments are located only on the rear sides, consider strapping the car seat in using the car's safety belts.

However if you can't secure the seat firmly in the center, use a side seat. If you have more than one child riding in the backseat, use side seats or place one child in the center rear seat and the other on the right rear seat. That way you can see her more easily and get her in and out of the car from the right side if you're parked on a busy street.

Beware swivel seats. Never place a car seat on a swivel or pull-down seat or on a rear- or side-facing seat, the kind sometimes found in station wagons, SUVs, and motor homes.

Tighten up. According to National Safe Kids Campaign, four out of five car seats are used incorrectly, and according to car-seat inspectors, the most common mistake is that the seats are too loose.

To check yours, grab the car seat at the base, near where your car's safety belt passes through the seat. Try to move the seat left, right, and forward. If it moves more than 1 inch (2 cm) in any direction, it's too loose. To tighten it, kneel on the seat and put all of your weight into it. (Use your arm for an infant seat.) Tighten the seat belt as much as possible and lock the belt. (Check your car manual if you're not sure how to do this.)

If your car was made before 1996, the belt might not lock enough, and you'll need to use a locking clip. Most car seats come with one.

Check the car seat angle. Rear-facing seats should be at a 45-degree angle to help keep your baby's airway open and cushion her back and neck. If the seat is too upright, your baby's head could fall forward, cutting off her airway so she can't breathe. Many seats have built-in levels to tell you if the angle is correct. If yours doesn't, here's an easy way to check yourself: Take a square piece of paper. Fold it corner to corner to form a triangle. Place the longest part of the triangle against the back of the car seat, where your baby's back goes. (That's the hypotenuse; betcha didn't think you'd ever need to know that past tenth grade geometry!) The top edge of the triangle should be parallel with the ground. If you have a level on hand, you could use that to check for sure.

If you need to adjust the angle, adjust the seat's adjustable pedestal. If your seat doesn't have one, place a tightly rolled up towel under the area of the car seat where the baby's feet rest to tilt the seat back more.

Stick to the rear. "Keep your baby rear-facing as long as possible, at least until she is one year old and 20 pounds [9 kg], but better until she exceeds the car seat manufacturer's height or weight limit," says Sinclair. "Parents tend to move their babies to forward-facing too soon because they want to be able to look in their rearview mirrors and see that they are okay. We need that reassurance. But babies' neck muscles aren't developed, and rear-facing offers additional protection. It's interesting to note that in Sweden, kids ride rear-facing until they're four years old."

Switch-a-roo. When you move your child's car seat from rear- to front-facing, make these adjustments. (Check your seat's manual to be sure.)

- Move the shoulder straps to the slots that are at or above the child's shoulders. On many seats, the top harness slots must be used when the seat is forward-facing. The upper slots have extra reinforcement to keep the harness secure in a crash once the seat faces forward.
- Move the seat from the reclined to the upright position if required by the seat's manufacturer.
- Move the seat belt to run through the forward-facing belt path.

Don't accessorize. "Don't add after-market accessories—such as seat belt covers, buckle positioners, and neck supporters—to your car seat or seat belt unless they're recommended by the manufacturer," says Sinclair. "This includes items that are marketed to improve safety. There are no federal standards for these items. Also, the key is these things should not be needed. If for example, your child's seat belt doesn't fit her tightly, she doesn't need a buckle positioner, she probably needs to be in a booster seat instead."

Buckle up carefully. When you put your child into her car seat, make sure the harness straps aren't twisted, then pull the harness tight enough that you can't pinch any harness fabric between your fingers, and you can fit only one finger underneath the harness. Place the shoulder straps over your child's collar bones and the lap strap low on her hips. Slide the plastic retainer clip that holds the two straps together up to her armpit level. After you buckle your child in, tug the straps to make sure they're locked.

Stay firm. Around ten months, your baby may develop a rebellious streak and resist being strapped into her car seat. Don't give in. It's important to buckle her in each and every time.

Use the right slots. Most convertible car seats have several harness slots to adjust to your growing baby. The correct slots to use are the ones level with or slightly below your child's shoulders for rear-facing seat and level with or slightly above the shoulders for forward-facing seats.

Stay warm. Don't put your child into her car seat all bundled up in winter clothes. Remove the coat first. Similarly, don't cover her in a blanket before buckling her in. Buckle her in first, then cover her and the restraint with a blanket.

Prevent buckle burns. Before leaving your parked car on a hot day, cover or hide the metal latches to prevent the sun from hitting them directly. Your child could get burned from the hot metal.

Fill in helpers. "Ensure that everyone your child rides with in a car secures her in the car properly," says Sinclair. "Never allow your child to ride unrestrained, such as when being transported by a grandparent, the nanny, or in a carpool."

ATTENDING A CAR SEAT CLINIC

"Once you install your car seat, have it checked," says Alexander Sinclair, a highway safety specialist with the National Highway Traffic Safety Administration. To find a certified inspection location near you, visit www.seatcheck.org or call 866-SEAT-CHECK.

Inspections are free and take only about 20 minutes.

Replace the seat. If a car seat is in a moderate or severe crash, replace it. If the crash was minor—the vehicle was driven away from the crash, the vehicle door closest to the car seat wasn't damaged, no one in the vehicle was injured, the air bags didn't go off, and you don't see any damage to the car seat—it might not need to be replaced.

Ask for help. If you notice a problem with your car seat, or even if you think you notice a problem with your car seat, report it to the NHTSA at 888-DASH-2-DOT or 888-327-4236, says Sinclair. NHTSA will look into it and may even recall the seat if there's a serious problem with it.

Get company. If your child requires constant attention, have another adult drive with you so you can keep your eyes—and attention—on the road.

Choosing the Safest Car

Drive the safest car you can afford. Sure it's not practical to buy a new car just because a baby's on the way. But if you happen to find yourself in the market, here are some safety features to look for:

- Anti-roll control: This feature is mainly available in SUVs. It detects skids and tilts that could signal an impending rollover and then computerized controls take over.

- Antilock brakes: These brakes allow the driver to steer while braking hard.

- Auto reverse windows: If these windows are closing, they automatically go back down if something—such as a child's finger—gets in the way. These sensors are common in Europe, but they're required in the United States only in vehicles with one-touch-up windows and remotely controlled windows.

- Backup cameras: These let you see what's behind you while backing up.

- Child-safety locks: When engaged, these locks prevent your child—or anyone else for that matter—from opening the car door from the inside.

  "One day, I'm sorry to say, my son, Evan, opened the car door while I was driving," says Marie Suszynski, a mother of one and freelance writer in Emmaus, Pennsylvania. "Luckily I could turn onto a side street right away and pull over. Now I have a bigger car, and I don't think he can even reach the door handle while in his car seat. And if he does reach it, he can't open it because of the child safety locks. Of course, that hasn't stopped him from using his toes to put the window up and down!"

- Conversation mirror: This large mirror sits above the rearview mirror and provides a wide-angle view of the backseat. They're standard in Honda Odysseys and Ford Freestyles. They're safe because you're used to glancing in your rearview mirror, so looking at the additional one is an easy adjustment.

- Side-curtain air bags: These bags deploy from the ceiling to provide head protection during side-impact collisions.

- Side-impact air bags: These air bags deploy from the doors or the seat cushions to protect the torso area of adults during side-impact collisions.

- Sliding second-row seat: These seats slide forward, making it easier to pass things back to your child. They're standard in the Toyota Sienna 8 passenger, Volvo XC90 SUV, and Ford Expedition.

- Stability control: These sensors detect skidding, hydroplaning, or other losses of control and help the vehicle recover by automatically using the brakes and throttle.

MY SAFETY STORY

My daughter is nineteen years old now. She was an infant before there were seat belt inspection stations and such an emphasis on car seat and booster seat safety (and before I worked for the National Highway Traffic Safety Administration!). My wife and I were vigilant about securing our daughter into her car seat. But as often happens, after awhile, her car seat needed a good cleaning. I took it apart to clean it and discovered I'd need a degree in structural engineering to figure out how to put it back on. I read the instructions and did the best I could, but I was never sure I did it right. A few years later, my daughter graduated to a booster seat. We bought a common type at the time that's no longer sold— a shield booster seat. It had a shield that went across my daughter's abdomen, but nothing went across her chest. The car's seat belt held the booster seat into the car, but not much was holding my daughter into the booster seat. Thankfully, nothing happened. But I'm grateful that today there are seat belt inspectors, safety websites, and lots of information out there to help parents. Today's parents are not alone!

—Alexander Sinclair, a highway safety specialist with the
National Highway Traffic Safety Administration

Pass on this. One safety feature of cars to skip is the LCD video monitor. These interior video cameras project images of the backseat onto a screen in a rear-view mirror. This is great in theory because you can see what your rear-facing baby is doing, but the TV can distract you from the road.

Check out www.motherproof.com. If you're looking for a new car, this website offers informative reviews, from a mother-of-two's perspective. It includes some specifications of the cars and NHTSA crash test ratings as well.

Rethink SUVs. A study from Children's Hospital of Philadelphia found that children are no safer in SUVs than in cars. As it turns out, SUVs are more than twice as likely to roll over in crashes. Children are three times more likely to be injured in rollover crashes than in nonrollover crashes.

If you drive an SUV, check your tire pressure monthly and don't overload it.

Stress seat belt safety. Once your toddler is able to buckle and unbuckle her own seat, explain that you will not drive unless she is buckled up. Be prepared for her to test you on it. If she unbuckles while you're still driving, safely pull the car over and stop. Wait until she buckles back up before moving the car again.

Lock up. It's a great habit to get into: Lock your car doors while driving.

If your car has them, engage the child-safe locks. They prevent the backseat doors from being opened from the inside.

Take care with automatic windows. If your toddler puts her head or hand out the window and then accidentally leans on the window switch, the window can close on her. If your power windows have one, use the lock-out function so your child can't operate them from the backseat. Before you raise a window, look back to make sure all body parts are inside the car.

Stow packages in the trunk. "Don't leave unsecured items in your car. Put them in the trunk instead," says Sinclair. "Any loose item—even a tissue box or a book—can become a projectile in a crash, and its weight times its speed becomes the mass it will hit someone at."

Give babies soft toys only in the car. Cloth books or small stuffed animals are best while riding in a car. Harder, larger toys can become dangerous in a crash.

Watch your speed. "Most crash tests are done at 30 to 35 miles per hour, and even at these relative lower speeds, severe damage and injuries can occur," says Sinclair. "Just imagine what happens at 55, 60, 65, plus miles an hour. Speed is a huge issue on our roadways."

Avoid the dashboard diner. Don't give your child food to eat in the car. If she chokes, you might not be able to react quickly enough.

Safety Supplies: Sun Shades

Removable sun shade screens for your car's side windows will shade your baby from the sun. They'll keep the inside of your car from getting too hot also. Because peel and stick shades are more secure than those that attack with suction cups, they're safer. They cost between $12 and $20 through baby safety supplies catalogs.

Take along emergency numbers. Tuck a piece of paper in your car's glove compartment with phone numbers for the fire department, police department, ambulance services, your baby's pediatrician's office and after-hours number, poison control, and a neighbor.

Bring the baby inside. Never leave a child alone in a vehicle, even sleeping in her car seat in the garage. Any number of terrible things can happen: Temperatures in a car can reach deadly levels in minutes; a child can be strangled by power windows, sunroofs, or accessories; a child can be taken during a carjacking or kidnapped from the vehicle; or a child could knock the vehicle into gear, setting it into motion.

"Parents must be vigilant with kids around cars. Teach your kids that cars aren't toys," says Sinclair. The NHTSA is noticing an increase in problems with children around cars, and not necessarily as passengers, for example, children left alone in cars who get hypothermia or hyperthermia, who accidentally pop older cars into gear, who climb into the trunks of cars, and who are backed over in driveways, garages, and parking lots. These tragedies happen all too often.

Pack a first-aid kit. Keep a first-aid kit in your car. (See "Assembling a First-Aid Kit" on page 31.)

Prevent carbon monoxide poisoning. Clean out snow from your car's tailpipe before using the car. If you have an attached garage, don't warm the car inside it.

Keep car keys away from kids. Lock your car so that kids can't get inside and get locked in the car or trunk.

Safety Supplies: Trunk Release Mechanisms

Cars after model year 2002 have glow-in-the-dark release handles in their trunks that you can pull to release the trunk lids. Older cars, however, do not.

You could have a trunk release mechanism installed in your car so that a child could escape from the trunk. Or you can go to www.aablelocksmiths.com to buy the Quick-Out Emergency Trunk Release for around $15.

Safety Supplies: Backup Sensors, Rear-View Cameras, and Mirrors

Every 4 hours, a child in the United States is hit by a driver backing up in a driveway or parking lot. According to Kids and Cars, blind spots can average from 12 feet (3.5 m) for a Honda Accord to 30 feet (9 m) for a Chevrolet Avalanche, and 50 feet (15.25 m) for short drivers.

Consider installing a backup sensor and alarm, which cost around $90, or a rear-view camera, which cost around $300.

For a low-tech alternative, consider a Rearview Safety Lens. This mirror sticks on with static electricity and gives you a wide-angle rear view. It costs around $20 through baby safety supplies websites.

Back up with care. According to Kids and Cars, in 2002, which is the latest statistic, at least fifty-eight children died from being backed over by motor vehicles. More than 60 percent of the time it was a parent or close relative at the wheel.

Be ultra careful when backing up your car, especially if you drive an SUV, as these have poor rear visibility and very large blind spots. Adjust your rear and side view mirrors to minimize your blind spot. Raise your seat so that you are sitting as high as is safe. Shorter drivers have larger blind spots. Make sure that you know where your children are when you back up. Go to www.kidsandcars.org to see how big your car's blind spot is.

At Other People's Homes

No matter how well babyproofed your home is, the other homes you'll visit with your baby—Grandma's, friends', and even hotels—likely are not.

"The toughest babyproofing challenge for us was going to people's homes that weren't babyproofed and we weren't familiar with," says Leslie Keefe, a mother of one in Bethlehem, Pennsylvania. Our son, Kieran, would want to explore things, and we had to keep him contained. That's not easy for an eighteen-month-old!"

Make a list. When you're going to be away from home, take a list of contact names and numbers and your child's health information.

Call ahead. Find out whether your accommodations can be babyproofed before you arrive (possible at Grandma's, unlikely at a hotel). If not, bring your own babyproofing kit, including door knob covers, outlet covers, and pipe cleaners or twisties to secure draperies and electrical cords. Masking tape is very helpful also. You can use it to cover outlets, fasten a piece of cloth to soften a sharp table corner, attach an electrical cord to the floor, and secure cabinet doors.

If you're going to be staying too long to make it practical to simply watch your toddler like a hawk, ask if you can babyproof one room, moving furniture around to create a play space.

Bring a monitor. Take along a portable battery-operated monitor to keep tabs on your baby when you're not in the same room. Some monitors even have transmitters, not just receivers, that are battery operated.

Bring a kit. Put together a travel kit, including the first-aid kit you hopefully already have in your car, liquid acetaminophen, and rehydrating solution such as Pedialyte.

Pack a play yard. Look for collapsible ones that are easy to pack up. These are handy for your child to sleep in, to play in, and to keep him safe from pets. They provide instant, child-safe areas in homes that otherwise might not be babyproofed.

Consider a portable bassinet. Hotels may not have cribs available, and if they do, they might not be safe. In 2000, the National Safe Kids Campaign found unsafe cribs in 82 percent of the hotels and motels it visited. Portable bassinets and cradlettes let you set your baby up close to you.

If your baby will be sleeping in another crib, check that it is safe. (See "Choosing the Safest Crib" on page 13.)

Check out smoke alarms. Check to make sure that every home your child visits has working smoke alarms in every sleeping area and on every level.

SAFETY ON THE GO

Bring your own "crib" for your baby. You know that your own play yard meets safety standards, but you can't always be sure when borrowing one from a hotel or a friend away from home.

Pack your own monitor to keep tabs on your baby.

Be prepared in case your baby falls ill or gets injured.

For peace of mind, bring your own babyproofing kit, including door knob covers, outlet covers, and twist-ties to secure draperies and electrical cords.

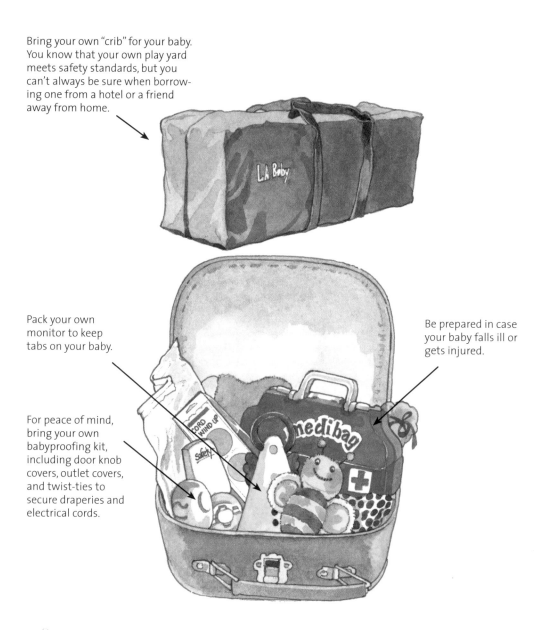

When you are away from home, you will likely find yourself in non-babyproofed environments. Plan ahead and bring along some key items to make your life on the road with your baby easier and safer.

Be obvious. Check the home or hotel room for obvious dangers, such as medications on end tables and kitchen knives within reach.

Ask about guns. "Before your child goes to a friend's house to play, make sure the home is safe," says Karen Sheehan, M.D., M.P.H., medical director of the Injury Prevention and Research Center at Children's Memorial Hospital in Chicago. "It can be awkward to ask questions; you might worry that they feel you don't trust them. But you don't want something terrible to happen either. It can be easiest to turn the question around to yourself. For example you could say, 'My husband likes to hunt so we have a gun in the home. However, to keep little Johnnie safe, my husband always stores the bullets away from the gun and locked up.' And then ask, 'Do you have a gun? What do you do to keep your family safe?'"

"If your child goes to a friend's house to play, ask if they have a gun and how it is secured," says Garry Gardner, M.D., a pediatrician in private practice in Darien, Illinois, and former member of the American Academy of Pediatrics Committee on Injury, Violence, and Poison Prevention. "If there is a gun and it is not secure, I would not let my children play there."

Watch out for windows. It's important to keep window covering safety in mind when visiting other places as well, such as other people's homes, vacation properties, and businesses. They might be even more likely to have old, potentially dangerous window treatments. Keep your child away from them. "And consider suggesting that they replace or retrofit their blinds," says Michael Cienian, vice president of quality and engineering for Springs Window Fashions and president of the Window Covering Safety Council.

Everywhere Else

Oh, the places you'll go with your child—to parks, malls, grocery stores, beaches, and more. Here's how to keep her safe when you venture out and about.

Stay in view. A small child won't understand the concept of staying in your view. Instead, teach her to stay where she can see you.

Know your name. Once your child is able to talk, teach her your first and last name and tell her to yell your name—instead of "Mom!" or "Dad!"—if you get separated. Explain that if she yells Mom or Dad, she'll have the attention of every mom and dad in the square block.

Be aware. Wherever you are with your baby, be aware of your surroundings. For example, in case of an emergency in a store, such as a fire, keep in mind how you got into the store and if possible locate an alternate exit.

Take a picture. Use your digital camera to take a photo of your toddler at the start of a day trip. That way if she gets lost, you have a photo that shows her in the clothes she's wearing that day.

Dress right. Dress your child in something recognizable and/or easy to remember, such as a bright orange T-shirt. If you have more than one child, when you go out, dress them in similar outfits. That way, if one child gets lost, it'll be easy for you to describe what she's wearing.

Safety Supplies: Who's Shoes ID

These tiny ID packets attach to a child's shoes. They include space for your child's name, contact information, and medical information and attach with Velcro. They cost around $8 at www.whosshoesid.com.

OUTDOOR SAFETY

Consider using a harness for toddlers and preschoolers.

Keep your children near: Use the restroom together; do not leave one to search for the other. Keep your eyes on them at all times.

Dress your children in bright, recognizable colors so they don't blend into the crowd.

Clever ID packets that attach to a child's shoes with Velcro are now available.

Young children wander off in public places every day. Bewildered parents are known to say, "But I looked away only for a second!" Take safety measures to make sure this doesn't happen to you.

Safety Supplies: Child Harnesses

According to the U.S. Department of Justice, more than 2,000 children are reported missing every day. Thankfully most of these children are recovered quickly.

To keep your child within arm's reach, consider using a harness. They cost around $13 in baby safety supplies catalogs.

Carry a photo. Always keep an up-to-date photo of your child in your wallet. This is helpful to show security or police in case she gets lost.

Help your child recognize dangerous situations. It seems so simple to tell kids "don't talk to strangers." But to a child that's a difficult concept to grasp. Plus, children told not to talk to strangers won't know who to turn to if they need help.

According to the Power of Parents Child Safety and Awareness Program, instead teach your child to be on the lookout for anyone she doesn't know approaching her, asking her questions, or making her feel scared.

Explain to your child who strangers are by saying, "They're people you don't know." Explain to her that she should never talk to a stranger, but mention key exceptions such as a police officer or crossing guard, especially if she's in trouble.

Teach your child that if she gets lost, she should approach a police officer, a salesperson with a name tag, a person in an information booth, or a mother with children. Tell your child that you'll never send someone she doesn't know to pick her up.

Role play. Talking with your kids about stranger dangers is great. But it's best to practice safety, too. According to the National Center for Missing & Exploited Children, create "what if" scenarios with your child to make sure she understands safety messages and how to use them. Use teachable moments, such as when you are at the park or in the mall.

MAKING AN ID KIT

While it's important to have a photo of your child with you in case of emergencies, it's even better to have an ID kit at home, too. The photo should be a recent head-and-shoulders color photo taken indoors of your child in which you can clearly see her face. Along with the photo write her name, nickname, height, weight, sex, age, eye color, and identifying marks.

Digital photos are preferred because they can be quickly transmitted by law enforcement. If you use a digital photo, save it with the highest possible resolution, between 200 and 600 dpi. Store the photo on your computer's hard drive, but also keep a copy on CD. Have at least one hard copy as well.

The National Center for Missing & Exploited Children urges parents to update their child's photos and information every six months (less than half of parents who have an emergency have done this). Children grow so rapidly that outdated photos could actually hinder law enforcement officials during a search.

Mark the calendar twice a year. Go to www.powerofparentsonline.com to enroll for a free reminder service and download a free photo identification kit. And be sure to store the photo in a safe place, accessible only by you. Don't save the information or photo on a public database.

Safety Supplies: Child Locators

These two-part devices include a receiver that you clip onto your child's shoe or belt and a transmitter that you keep. When you press the button on your transmitter, the receiver sounds a high-decibel beep. It works up to 150 feet (45.5 m), even through concrete walls, and is water-resistant. They cost around $30 through baby safety supplies catalogs.

Be safe on escalators. In the past five years, more than 10,000 kids, many under age four, were hurt on escalators. To be safe, don't take strollers on escalators. Tie or tuck in any loose clothing that could get caught. Make sure your child holds the rail or your hand and stands in the middle of a step. Teach her when and how to step off or pick her up at the end.

Safety Supplies: Table Topper

These disposable placemats are handy for providing a sanitary eating surface when eating out. And they stay in place once you put them on the table. They cost around $10 for twenty at baby safety supplies stores.

Use hook-on chairs carefully. These types of chairs are handy when eating out in restaurants. They attach to the edge of a table. But you must use them carefully. Don't place the chair where the child's feet can push off on other chairs or table legs. Once you install the chair, check to make sure it's secure by pulling backward on it. Of course, use them only on sturdy tables!

Beware shopping carts. Many infant car seats lock onto shopping carts, and some shopping carts have built-in infant seats. These choices are not as safe as they seem. A baby can tip over and fall out of the cart. Instead of using these seats, use a stroller or baby carrier while shopping with your baby.

Buckle up. Always use the safety straps on grocery carts, which tip over very easily. Also, never allow your child to stand in the basket of a shopping cart or ride hanging on to the side of the cart.

Keep an eye out. Never leave your child unattended in a shopping cart. Besides the danger of falling out, someone could just roll her away.

Safety Supplies: Diaper Bridge

This portable changing station makes it easy to change your child's diaper on top of a sink, which is often the only flat surface in bathrooms in places such as restaurants. It unfolds with one hand and fits in most diaper bags. They cost around $40 at www.diaperbridge.com or some baby specialty stores.

Pack a car seat. It might not always be practical, but when you can, bring along a car seat for public transportation, such as taxis, buses, and trains. Even when there are no seat belts to strap the car seat in, it will provide some protection for your child.

Buy a seat. Although most airlines let kids under age two fly free, it's best to buy your baby her own seat. If you encounter turbulence, she'll be far safer buckled into her own car seat.

Fly the friendly skies. The American Academy of Pediatrics and the Federal Aviation Administration (FAA) recommend that children should sit in car seats on planes until they are four years old. Most infant, convertible, and forward-facing seats are certified to be used on planes. Look for a note of FAA-approval on your seat or check with your seat's manufacturer to be sure. Generally, car seats that are no wider than 16 inches (40.5 cm) fit best on airplane seats.

The FAA recently certified AmSafe CAReS (Child Aviation Restraint System), a web-buckle device that takes the place of a front-facing seat, for kids over age one between 20 and 45 pounds (9 and 20.5 kg). It attaches to the regular seat belt. Airlines may offer it in the future.

Most airlines let kids under age two fly free without a designated seat, but it's best to buy your baby her own seat and bring along a certified-for-air-travel car seat. The American Academy of Pediatrics and the Federal Aviation Administration both recommend that children under age four sit in car seats on planes.

Check the temperature. If you take your child swimming in a pool or lake, make sure the water is warm enough, between 84°F and 87°F (29°C and 30.5°C).

Spot a lifeguard. If you're swimming at a pool or beach, make sure it is supervised by a lifeguard, but don't rely on the lifeguard to supervise your child. Stay close enough to your child that you could grab her if need be. Position yourself on the deeper side of the water from your child.

Teach water safety. Warn your child about playing in fast moving water, such as rivers and canals, and never let young children play unsupervised near water, even if they know how to swim.

Wear a life jacket. Whenever riding in a boat or fishing, children need to wear a U.S. Coast Guard–approved life jacket. Water wings ant other air-filled swimming aids aren't the same as life jackets.

Look out for thin ice. Avoid walking, skating, or riding on weak or thawing ice on any body of water.

Go to toddler-safe playgrounds. Each year, 200,000 kids go to emergency rooms because of playground injuries, most of them falls and many of them because of insufficient supervision. Because most playground equipment is designed for kids ages two to five or six to twelve, children under two really don't belong on regular playgrounds. Look for special toddler playgrounds with infant swings. Or keep your little one off the playground equipment and in the sandbox or on the grass.

Be a spotter. Follow your child around the playground. That way you'll be close enough to catch her if she loses his footing and starts to fall. If the playground is too crowded, choose another spot.

Look down. Make sure that the playground your child plays in has loose-fill materials—such as hardwood mulch or chips, fine sand, or shredded rubber—around and under jungle gyms, slides, and swings. The fill should be 6 to 12 inches (15 to 30 cm) deep, and it should extend several feet in every direction around equipment. What shouldn't it be? Asphalt, concrete, grass, or packed dirt. Keep an eye out for hazards such as broken glass.

Be careful on equipment. Don't put your child on your lap to go down slides. Her legs or feet could get caught between your body and the slide. Don't let your child get to close to other kids swinging on wooden or metal seats, who could swing into her. Watch out for openings that are large enough for a child to get her head or limbs caught in. If it's very hot outside, use playground equipment only early in the morning, before the sun heats it up.

Wash up. If you take your child to a petting zoo, keep her hands out of her mouth and don't let her eat anything until you wash her hands with soap and water. If that's not possible, use an alcohol-based hand gel. Baby wipes won't do the trick. Animals can transmit intestinal infections such as *E. coli.*

Stay safe on kiddies rides. Before letting your child go on any rides at an amusement park, make sure she understands the rules. Falls are common on kiddies rides, so keep one hand on your child at all times.

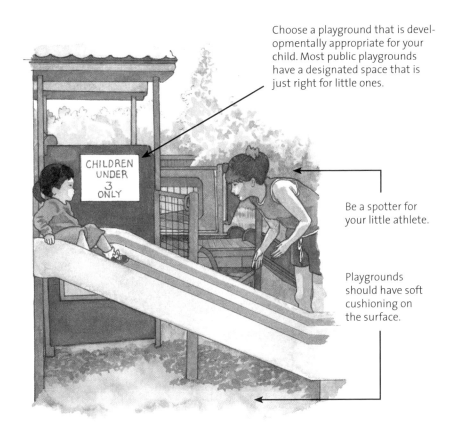

Choose a playground that is developmentally appropriate for your child. Most public playgrounds have a designated space that is just right for little ones.

CHILDREN UNDER 3 ONLY

Be a spotter for your little athlete.

Playgrounds should have soft cushioning on the surface.

It's not always fun and games at the playground. Be on the lookout for litter such as broken glass, hard concrete or asphalt surfaces under play areas, and hot spots on slides and jungle gyms. And don't forget the antibacterial wipes and/or alcohol-based hand gel before snack time: Playgrounds are notorious germ magnets!

RESOURCES

Check out the following organizations and websites for more information on safety.

American Academy of Pediatrics
141 Northwest Point Boulevard
Elk Grove Village, IL 60007
847-434-4000
www.aap.org

American Association of Poison Control Centers
3201 New Mexico Avenue, Suite 330
Washington DC 20016
202-362-7217
Poison Control Emergency Hotline: 800-222-1222
www.1-800-222-1222.info

American Red Cross
2025 E Street NW
Washington DC 20006
202-303-4498
www.redcross.org

American Society for Testing and Materials
100 Barr Harbor Drive, PO Box C700
West Conshohocken, PA 19428-2959
610-832-9585
www.astm.org

Center for Environmental Health
528 61st Street, Suite A
Oakland, CA 94609-1204
510-594-9864
www.cehca.org

First Candle/SIDS Alliance
1314 Bedford Avenue, Suite 210
Baltimore, MD 21208
800-221-7437
www.sidsalliance.org

Home Safety Council
1250 Eye Street, NW, Suite 1000
Washington DC 20005
202-330-4900
www.homesafetycouncil.org

Juvenile Products Manufacturers Association
15000 Commerce Parkway, Suite C
Mt. Laurel, NJ 08054
856-638-0420
www.jpma.org

Kids and Cars
2913 West 113th Street
Leawood, KS 66211
913-327-0013
www.kidsandcars.org

Kids In Danger
116 W. Illinois Street, Suite 5E
Chicago, IL 60610-4522
312-595-0649
www.kidsindanger.org

National Center for Missing & Exploited Children
699 Prince Street
Alexandria, VA 22314-3175
703-274-3900
24-Hour Hotline: 800-THE-LOST (800-843-5678)
www.missingkids.com

National Center on Shaken Baby Syndrome
2955 Harrison Boulevard, #102
Ogden, UT 84403
888-273-0071
www.dontshake.com

National Fire Protection Association
1 Batterymarch Park
Quincy, MA 02169-7471
617-770-3000
www.nfpa.org

National Highway Traffic Safety Administration
1200 New Jersey Avenue, SE, West Building
Washington DC 20590
888-327-4236
www.nhtsa.dot.gov

Parents Television Council
707 Wilshire Boulevard, #2075
Los Angeles, CA 90017
800-882-6868
www.parentstv.org

Power of Parents
www.powerofparentsonline.com

Safe Kids Worldwide
1301 Pennsylvania Avenue, NW, Suite 1000
Washington DC 20004
202-662-0600
www.safekids.org

Safe Playgrounds Project
528 61st Street, Suite A
Oakland, CA 94609
800-652-0827
www.safe2play.org

SeatCheck
866-SEAT-CHECK
www.seatcheck.org

U.S. Consumer Product Safety Commission
4330 East West Highway
Bethesda, MD 20814
800-638-2772
www.cpsc.gov

U.S. Environmental Protection Agency
1200 Pennsylvania Avenue, NW
Washington DC 20460
National Lead Information Center: 800-424-5323
Safe Drinking Water Hotline: 800-426-4791
www.epa.gov

Underwriters Laboratories
333 Pfingsten Road
Northbrook, IL 60062-2096
847-272-8800
www.ul.com

Window Covering Safety Council
355 Lexington Avenue, Suite 1500
New York , NY 10017
800-506-4636
www.windowcoverings.org

Acknowledgments

I am grateful for the support and help of many people, without whom this book wouldn't have been possible. Thank you to my friend and mentor Ellen Phillips, wonderfully supportive managing editor John Gettings, editor Cara Connors, project manager Amanda Waddell, copy editor Kelly Ahlquist, proofreader Kathy Dragolich, indexer Judy Kip, designer Rachel Fitzgibbon, and illustrator Wendy Edelson.

Thank you also to the many experts and parents who shared their tips and stories with me.

Most of all thank you to my family—Mike Reich, Tyler Reich, Austin Reich, John Richard Bright, Mary Bright, and Robyn Swatsburg—for being a constant source of love and support.

About the Author

Jennifer Bright Reich has worked in publishing for more than ten years, spending time as both a project editor for Rodale Inc. and as a freelance writer and editor. She has contributed to more than 150 books and has published nearly 100 newspaper and magazine articles. She also runs her own website, www.DisneyWithKids.net, which helps families traveling to Walt Disney World save money, time, and sanity.

Jennifer lives in a highly babyproofed home in Hellertown, Pennsylvania, with her husband and their two young sons.

INDEX

L

LATCH (Lower Anchors and Tethers for Children) system, 205–206
latex balloons, avoiding, 133
laundry chute, 171
laundry, UV protection and, 188
lawn chemicals, 153
lawn mower, 151
lead
  in paint, 27, 37, 38
  in pottery, 107
  in water, 65
litter box, 147
living room safety
  birth to six months, 74–77
  six months to one year, 128–135
  toddlers, 173
locators, for children, 225
look-alikes, 101, 119, 149

M

magnets, 137
manuals, 22
matches, 134
mattress, for crib, 13–14, 54, 55, 95, 159
medicine
  displaying record of dosage, 60
  disposing of properly, 120
  giving age-appropriate dose, 69
  giving in light, not dark, 69
  keeping out of reach, 119, 171
  reading label on, every time, 29
microwave, avoiding use of, 65
mineral oil, 120
mold, checking for, 45
motherproof.com, 212
motorized pool covers, 195
movement sensors, 18

N

nail trimming, 69
name, teaching toddler your, 221
nap, in crib, 75
National Highway Traffic Safety Administration contact information, 202, 209
nightlights, 15, 42
noise, of toys, 98
"no," use of, 177, 190
nursery
  before birth, 12–19
  birth to six months, 52–57

six months to one year, 94–99
toddlers, 158–161
nuts, avoiding, 115

O

organic baby food, 113
outdoor safety
  birth to six months, 84–91
  six months to one year, 148–155
  toddlers, 184–197
outlet covers, 142–143

P

pacifier, 54, 55, 59, 175
paint, 27, 37, 38, 153
papers, keeping out of reach, 133, 143
pasteurization, 116
Pendleton, Angel, 102, 122
pets. *See* dogs and cats
petting zoo, 229
photograph, keeping recent for identification, 89, 221, 223, 224
plagiocephaly, 77
plants, poisonous, 129, 153, 155
plastic bags, 81, 143
plastic wrap, 97
playgrounds, toddler-safe, 228–229
play yard, 26–27, 75, 133
  for travel, 217, 218
Poison Control Center telephone number, 120
poisoning. *See* food poisoning, plants; toxins
poison ivy, 196
pool
  alarms for, 196–197
  fencing for, 192
  motorized covers for, 195
  safety tips for, 193–194
positive attitude, 177
potpourri, 132
pottery, lead in, 107
power strip covers, 142
pregnancy, cats and, 48–49
"Preparing Fido," 48
pressure-treated wood, 150, 152
purses, keeping out of reach, 110
PVC, 22